The House that Disappeared on Tory Island

By Anton McCabe

The **Drumkeen** Press

The House that Disappeared on Tory Island
First Published September 2012
By
The Drumkeen Press
7 Sunningdale
Omagh
Co Tyrone
BT78 1JX
Northern Ireland

Email: thedrumkeenpress@hotmail.co.uk

Copyright © Anton McCabe 2012

ISBN: 978-0-9553552-2-6

All rights reserved. The material in this publication is protected by copyright law. Except as may be permitted by law, no part of the material may be reproduced (including storage in a retrieval system) or transmitted in any form or by any means; adapted; rented or lent without the written permission of the copyright owners. Applications for permission should be addressed to the publisher.

The moral right of the author has been asserted.

Printed in Ireland by Browne Printers Ltd, Letterkenny. Co. Donegal.

DEDICATION

In memory of Bridget O'Toole-Walsh of Gleneely, Co. Donegal, who died on November 11th 2011. A remarkable woman, friend and comrade.

Acknowledgements

With grateful thanks to all those who helped make this book a reality. In particular, Michael Gillespie, Bridget O'Toole-Walsh, Dolores Meenan, The Drumkeen Press and the people of Tory Island who chose to speak up.

Anton McCabe is from Omagh, Co. Tyrone. He is a freelance journalist who has contributed to a wide variety of print and broadcast outlets, in both English and Irish.

He is a member of the Irish Executive Committee of the National Union of Journalists.

Photograph courtesy of JIM DUNNE

Chapter One

As the ferry set its course for the harbour on Tory Island, Neville Presho stood in the prow keen to get his first look at the house he had left behind eight years before when he left for New Zealand. His wife, Fiona, made the more comfortable choice of sitting in the cabin with their two young children. It was a perfect July day in 1994. The sea off the Donegal coast was calm, the air clear. Neville was excited that he was going to see his house again. Even better, he was going to show both it and Tory to Fiona. The island was a special place to Neville.

The family would stay in the house. Neville and Fiona were considering making it their home, if they were to return to live in Ireland. The house had character. It was about 150 years old, one of the oldest on the island. The walls were three feet thick and built from stone. There were two storeys, and six bedrooms. Neville was expecting to see some damage as, two months beforehand, he had received a letter from Donegal County Council to say it was in a dangerous condition due to storm damage. Despite this, he assumed it would be habitable – at least for the few days the family was going to spend on the island.

From out at sea, Neville could make out the shape of a white building in the general area of his house. He took it for granted that the shape was his house because he had whitewashed it before leaving. All was well. However, as the boat approached the harbour, Neville saw the white building was some big, new construction that had not existed when he was last on Tory. It stood behind where his house had been. Of the house, there was not a sight. 'It was a huge shock. It flicked a switch in my brain,' he recalled later. Neville rushed into the cabin and kept repeating to Fiona: 'It's gone, the house is gone.'

When the boat docked, he walked up Tory's one street. What he came upon was beyond his understanding: 'Where my house had been there was a vacant space, with large boulders round it delineating a car park. I'm talking about ten feet by ten feet, painted white. Not only was the site vacant but where my septic tank had been running north-south, there was another one, identical, except it was running east-west. Also, where mine was solid concrete on top, the new one had strips of concrete on top.'

As Neville searched, he came upon some traces of his house. There was a foot-long piece of black plastic pipe sticking up above the ground. That pipe had once supplied water to his house. Upside down on the foreshore below where the house had stood, there lay a rusting bath – Neville's bath.

Beside where the house had been, and right across the road from the island's church, there was a patch of ground with rubble dumped on it. Neville looked at the rubble and recognized bits of concrete as having come from the porches of his house. He also noticed some stones of a roughly square shape that had come from a building; and realized they had once been the walls of his house.

The Island's new hotel, Ostán Thoraigh, had been opened in May that year, and stood straight across the road from where his house had been. In his confusion, Neville did not note that, had his house still existed, it would have blocked the hotel's view of the sea and the mainland. For now, Neville's immediate need was to find out what grotesque, unbelievable, bizarre and unprecedented catastrophe had swept it away. Neville knew the owner of Ostán Thoraigh, so it was to him he first turned for help. After all, he had known Patrick Doohan for the best part of 20 years. As a teenager, Patrick had taken part in the film about Tory that Neville had made in 1976 – "Oileán/An Island". Over the years since, they had always been, if not friends, at least friendly.

'We went in to the hotel to see Patrick Doohan,' Neville remembered. 'In my wife's presence, I said "What would you do in my situation?" That was all we asked him. "I'd want to find out who burnt your house," he said.'

With no house to stay in, the Preshos booked into a B&B. Neville set to asking islanders what had happened. For nearly a decade from the late 70s, he had lived part of the year on Tory; he loved the community, and felt that love was reciprocated. Now he found he was facing a wall of silence. No one he spoke to knew anything about his house, none had seen it being demolished, nor seen the car park and septic tank being built. Islanders he had come to know well were tight-lipped.

Only one let anything slip. He was one of the men Neville knew well. They met as Neville walked past the Round Tower. Neville asked him: 'Do you know anything about my house disappearing?' The man replied: 'It would be better if you didn't ask about that.'

The only person willing to talk to him was another outsider, island priest Fr Niall O'Neill. Fr O'Neill told Neville of waking in the early hours of

14th January 1993 and seeing a red glow in the sky. Assuming it was the aurora borealis, he went back to sleep. He awoke in the morning to find that Neville's house had been burnt out. It was then he realized that the red glow had come from the blaze.

After four days on the island, the Preshos returned to the mainland. But it was a different Neville who had returned from Tory

*   *   *

They were to spend another two months in Ireland during which time he became increasingly hyperactive, took to drinking heavily, and could not sleep. He was obsessed with finding out what had happened to his house. He travelled round Ireland 'like a blue-arsed fly' in his search for information. Where he asked questions, he felt doors were shut against him.

Before going to Tory, Neville had written to the County Council in response to their letter regarding his house. In his letter, Neville had asked four very precise questions:–

–Do you know the exact date of the fire?

–Was there a file report and, if so, could you send a copy?

–Was there a police report and if so, could you send a copy?

–Who are the owners of the new hotel who have expressed concern at the condition of the house?

The switch that flicked in Neville's brain when he found his house had disappeared meant he was never again able to write with such precision. He was so distressed he did not notice that the Council did not deal with these questions. An official with an illegible signature replied to him on behalf of the County Secretary: "I acknowledge receipt of your letter dated 5th inst concerning the condition of your house on Tory Island. We have received numerous complaints regarding the build (sic) and our Area Engineer subsequently submitted a report on same."

He went to the Planning Department of Donegal County Council at its offices in Lifford, to inquire if it had received any reports about the house. There he met with indifference. A senior Council official told him that the Council had no way of knowing what had happened on Tory as the Council did not have a presence on the island. In actual fact, an islander was employed by the Council as a multi-skilled operative on Tory during the entire period the house was disappearing.

On foot of Neville's inquiries, the then County Manager wrote to the Administrative Officer in the Housing Department: "While the Council will be as helpful as possible in respect of the aspects of the case that concern the Council, we will not become involved in the investigation of the alleged criminal activities."

The Manager also wrote to Neville: "I have a great admiration for the patience and tolerance which you have displayed having regard to the sequence of events as outlined by you in correspondence and discussions."

He then informed Neville that the Council "acted in good faith in everything which it did in relation to the matter." Subsequently, Neville made inquiries to the Council regarding compensation. That stung the Council into a direct and meaningful reply:

"You would not be entitled to claim compensation for this damage under the Malicious Injuries Act 1981 and 1986 since it would appear that it was not caused during a riot or was connected with the troubles in Northern Ireland. I regret the Council cannot be of assistance to you in the matter. Copies of the 1986 (Amendment) Act and relevant sections of the 1981 Act are enclosed for your information."

Seeking legal representation, Neville approached a solicitor he had used for his film business; the solicitor would not take up his case. Neville went on to apply for and receive outline planning permission to build a replacement house on the same site on Tory. However, so confused was his mental state that he proceeded no further. After five years went by without work commencing, this permission lapsed.

He sought assistance from the Gardaí. He went to a station to report what had happened, asking: 'What are you going to do about my house that has disappeared?' He later told the High Court that an officer replied: "I've better things to do than worry about your ould house on Tory Island." He gave more receptive Gardaí a video and photographs which showed the remains of the house bulldozed onto the foreshore.

He taped an interview with building contractor John McGinty regarding the burning. Two of McGinty's workmen had been living in the house until a couple of days before the fire, and McGinty himself had stayed there regularly in the months before the fire. All without Neville's knowledge. McGinty's memory was still very fresh at that stage. Neville posted the tape to the Gardaí; in the course of years, the tape has disappeared.

However, not all of Neville's activities proved fruitless. He hired an engineer, Albert Fry, to draw up a structural report to determine what had befallen the house. This report was based on photos Neville had obtained from Donegal County Council. It would be another 15 years before his case reached the High Court; the evidence of the photographs and Fry's report were central to that happening.

As his two months in Ireland passed, Neville came to realize the disappearance of the house was changing his personality:

'Basically, the first thing what happened to the house did to me, I started feeling this churning in my stomach. The only way I could get rid of it was drinking copious quantities of alcohol. I changed as a person and became a different kind of person. This was something my wife had never experienced before. I didn't drink much before. I took a social drink to pass myself. But to get rid of this churning feeling, I had to anaesthetise it with alcohol.'

*   *   *

In September, Neville and his family returned to his job as a landscape gardener in Queenstown on New Zealand's South Island. It was spring there.

Queenstown, with its lakes and mountains, seemed a paradise after the stress of the previous two months.

That peace was not to last. Neville recalls:

'Two weeks after I came back, I was working away one day, I felt I was going out of my mind. I dashed to the doctor and asked him: "Am I certifiable? I think I'm going out of my mind." '

The doctor sent Neville to the mental health ward in Southland Hospital, Inverrcargil. It was his first time in hospital for mental illness. In the hospital he was diagnosed as suffering from bipolar disorder. Doctors initially considered his account of the disappearance of the house, and of having been a film-maker, as proof of serious mental illness. They were shocked when Fiona confirmed that this was truly Neville's past.

Neville did not find the hospital experience too distressing. That was despite falling out with a young American doctor. The American sectioned him – that is, ordered that he be forcibly detained. For the first time, Neville was taken to a secure mental hospital, this one nearly 150 miles away in Dunedin. After a few days there, he was discharged. However, discharge did not mean cure. Neville's health was never to recover.

Prior to returning to New Zealand in September 1994, Neville had arranged to meet Garda Sergeant Friel in Donegal that November to further the investigation into the disappearance of his house. Instead, Neville wrote to the Sergeant asking him to stop the investigation. He also wrote to those he believed were guilty of the burning, telling them they had his unconditional forgiveness. The alleged culprits did not write back. Neville was not surprised: 'But then pigs don't fly in Ireland.'

His letter to Sergeant Friel was followed by a phone call to the same effect. This also let the Sergeant know that he, Neville, had had a premonition that the roof was to be blown off the hotel by an act of God. Sergeant Friel was sufficiently struck to make a note of this conversation as being 'peculiar', but the Gardaí ceased the investigation.

The decline in Neville's health was dramatic. In the 1980s he was one of Ireland's most talented filmmakers. After his experience of that day in July 1994, he would never be well enough to make another film. He found himself increasingly unable to work, unable to concentrate. Over the next 15 years, he would be admitted to psychiatric hospitals eight times. On two occasions, he would be sectioned. Because of his illness, his marriage would break up. His four children would lose their father.

Fiona has summed up what that July day did to Neville, her and their family: 'To me it appeared that hell had been let loose in our family after that because of the change in Neville's mental state and his behaviour and the subsequent misfortunes which befell both of us.'

Chapter Two

For over 100 years, the house that became Neville's stood between Ward's Hotel and the sea. Ward's had been one of the most important buildings on Tory, and a physical link with history. The builders of the hotel had used stones from Tory's mediaeval monastery. Ward's was linked, too, with the Gaelic Revival of the early Twentieth Century; 1916 martyrs Patrick Pearse, Thomas McDonagh and Roger Casement had been guests.

In the early 20th Century, Ward's had also been a busy pub, shop and fish-merchants. After World War One, its businesses slipped into decline, to expire eventually during World War Two. The last Ward on the island died a decade later, in the 1950s. She left the building empty. The glories of its past faded away. By the 1990s, islanders were using the decaying building to store fishing nets and distil poitín.

The house that disappeared on Tory Island

That was until 1992, when a tall and vigorous Patrick Doohan swept back onto his home island bearing spectacular plans for economic development. A decade and a half before, a young fisherman whom the islanders called Patrick Eoin had headed off for the building sites of London. A confident businessman returned. Patrick had wealth – at least by the standards of a remote island – and a record of success in the outside world. The Irish economy was taking off, making it an excellent time for an ambitious man to return home – particularly a man promising a hotel that would put his home island on the tourist map. Patrick's vision of a new hotel convinced the Comharchumann (island cooperative) to sell him Ward's Hotel and the land surrounding it.

In June 1992, Patrick applied to the County Council for planning permission for the hotel. He sent the Council a copy of the site notice:– "Take notice that I am applying to Donegal County Council for planning permission to erect a hotel on this my land." Patrick did not complete the purchase of the site until five months later. He said the application involved "part retained, part demolition" of Ward's property. The planners declared the application invalid because the documentation was not complete.

Patrick mobilized political support from Fine Gael TD, Dinny McGinley. McGinley wrote twice to the Donegal County Manager in support of Patrick's application:– "I would be grateful if you could let me know what is the up-to-date position regarding same."

Patrick produced the required documents in July, and the planners got to work. The documents showed that he planned to demolish most of Ward's building. The plans also showed Neville's house directly in front of the proposed hotel.

Question 7(d) of the planning application form asked:– "Are all...septic tanks etc. within 100 yards radius of the development, marked approximately on the location map?"

Neville's septic tank was not shown despite being only about 30 yards from where the front door of the new hotel was planned to be sited. It was not marked on the location map supplied to the Council, and no planning officials noticed it during their inspections. That same Council, on the 10th November 1992, granted permission for a fourteen-bedroom hotel to be built on Ward's old property.

On the 9th November 1992, the Comharchumann completed the purchase of Ward's, prior to transferring it to Patrick. The following day, an Edward Naughton rang Neville's solicitor in Dublin and offered to buy Neville's house. The solicitor wrote to Neville on the 10th November saying Naughton represented "a Tory Island development unit". Edward Naughton was more widely known as Éamonn Ó Neachtain, and was then manager of the Comharchumann on Tory. Neville and Fiona were unsure if they would ever return to Ireland. They talked over the offer, and subsequently informed the Dublin solicitor they would be willing to sell for £7,000 (€8,890).

When Naughton/Ó Neachtain offered £1,000 (€1,270), Neville's solicitor did not feel the need to contact the Preshos. On the 16th December 1992, he informed Ó Neachtain the offer was 'ludicrous'. It has since emerged that the Comharchumann had, shortly before that, sold a house for £5,000 (€6,350).

In March 2009, Ó Neachtain gave evidence in the High Court that the Comharchumann had no particular plans for the house but saw the site as having great potential for development. Ó Neachtain also told the Court that the Comharchumann was working with Patrick in his plans for the hotel. However, there is no evidence that either Ó Neachtain or the Comharchumann were in any way involved in the destruction of the house.

Ward's had barely passed from the Comharchumann to Patrick when most of the old building was flattened and construction work began on Ostán Thoraigh. This was to be the only hotel on the island, and the most remote hotel in Ireland. It was situated a mere 100 feet from the shore. The only problem was that the stunning views of Tory Sound with the long ridge of Muckish and the sharp peak of Errigal beyond it, the high cliffs of Horn Head to the east and Arranmore Island far to the south-west, could not be seen by any of the paying guests. Instead they would have a close-up of the peeling walls and boarded-up windows of an old house; a house whose owner was an outsider who lived on the other side of the world, and had not been seen on Tory since 1986.

To build the hotel, Patrick had hired a building contractor from the mainland, John McGinty. Whilst the work lasted, McGinty and his workmen, John Friel and Brian Rodden, needed somewhere to stay. Because the islanders' attitude to private property was somewhat relaxed, that problem was soon resolved. Neville had left the keys of his house with an island woman when he left for the other side of the world. She gave the keys to McGinty so he and his men could stay there. To make that stay more comfortable, McGinty fixed up the bathroom and kitchen.

Building the hotel was not the only job McGinty alleged Patrick wanted him to do. McGinty would later give evidence in the High Court that Patrick offered him £1,000 (€1,270) to demolish Neville's house. Before undertaking this extra work, McGinty asked Patrick to provide proof of ownership. When this was not forthcoming, McGinty refused to touch the job.

McGinty had other jobs underway on the mainland, so did not stay on the island permanently. The house was roofed with asbestos sheeting and, during one of McGinty's absences, on the 11th January 1993, one of the sheets came away. This was unexpected because the position of the sheet was relatively sheltered. The missing sheet was on the side of the house that overlooked the sea. That is, it faced away from the site of the hotel on which Friel and Rodden were working. The sheet was on a part of the roof hidden from their view. It was just above the porch and within easy reach of anyone standing on its flat concrete roof.

When the two men returned to the house and found the damage, they informed McGinty. The contractor felt there was something happening that he did not like. In his experience, it was most unusual for an asbestos sheet in the middle of a roof to blow off. Normally, the sheets at the edges were the first to go.

There was just one other sheet of asbestos available on Tory. Its owner gave it to Friel and Rodden to repair the hole. The two set about doing this, helped by an elderly island man. Soon after they started work, Patrick appeared with his digger and offered assistance.

From the evidence given in the High Court in 2009, it appears that, at some stage during the attempt to repair the roof, the asbestos sheet fell. On the ground, it came into contact with the wheel of Patrick's digger and was broken. There was no evidence that the destruction was deliberate. However, the effect of this destruction was far-reaching.

With the only spare sheet of asbestos available on the island having been destroyed, it was not long before the wind tore other sheets off the roof and made a bigger hole. As a result, the house quickly became uninhabitable in a stormy, wet, cold January.

After two days, McGinty told Friel and Rodden to move out of the house and into the island's hostel. He instructed them to remove the electrical fuses from the fusebox in the porch before they left. In the subsequent fire, the porch was the only part of the house that was not burnt. This meant the fire was not caused by an electrical fault.

On the same day, 13th January 1993, that Rodden and Friel left Neville's house for the hostel, Patrick left the island. In 2009, he told the High Court his wife had had to be admitted to the hospital in Letterkenny on that evening.

By 3am on Thursday 14th January, the last islanders had gone to bed. They reported seeing nothing unusual. With nobody else afoot, the arsonists could take their time. It was a stormy night with the storm drowning out any noise. Once the fire was well lit, the wind fanned it with the hole in the roof acting as a chimney. Fr O'Neill was the only island resident disturbed, and that very briefly.

The fire was so fierce that it consumed every wooden part of Neville's house. Bales of fireproof cosywrap insulation that McGinty had stored in the house had melted. Only the stone walls were left standing. The fire was burnt out well before 7am.

To produce such an intense and rapid fire, an accelerant was needed. Diesel was readily available on the island. By 9am, when Friel and Rodden went down to the house, they found the embers smouldering. The charred remains of the boat Neville had built when he was seventeen lay among the debris. Burnt with the house were tools and building materials to the value of £5,000 (€6,350) belonging to McGinty. He, Friel and Rodden also lost clothes and bedclothes.

Fr. O'Neill noted in his diary that the fire was the talk of the island the next day. At the start, the islanders blamed an electrical fault. Within two days an elderly island woman comprehensively rubbished that story. She was famous as being able to ferret out the details of every happening on the island. She told Fr O'Neill that the door of Neville's house had been pushed in and the fire started in the downstairs storeroom, between bags of coal and gas cylinders. She did not divulge her sources.

On 15th January 1993, McGinty informed the Gardaí of the fire, and expressed the belief that it was arson. McGinty's style was always forthright. 'I rang up the Guards and said the house went on fire: "It's no fucking accident – this house was burnt"'.

The following day he followed up with another call in a similar vein. The contractor expected action would be taken. The Gardaí drew up a memo – "Disappearance of dwelling house at West Town, Tory Island."

Garda records contain a note confirming McGinty's second report, recording him as saying: "He was satisficd that the fire was malicious," and estimating the damage at £4,000 (€5,080). Action Taken was recorded as: "Particulars passed to Superintendent's office Glenties to arrange for scenes of crime man to visit island."

In December, Inspector James Gallagher from Glenties sent a letter headed "Dangerous Building on Tory Island" to Neville in New Zealand. Gallagher included a copy of the entry regarding McGinty's report in the Occurrence Book of Bunbeg Garda station. Inspector Gallagher said: "There was no Garda report made subsequently to this report. I trust this will be of assistance to you."

The Gardaí have blamed stormy weather for their failure to react to the fire. Gales blew for most of the week after the event. Only Monday 18th was clear, according to records at the Meteorological Station at Malin Head. The gales subsided after Tuesday 26th January. Even at that stage, a forensic examination would have been able to locate traces of accelerant in the ruins. Furthermore, by the early 1990s stormy weather did not completely isolate Tory. There was a fortnightly helicopter service, on alternate Thursdays. The helicopter made its fortnightly trip on 21st January, and a Garda could have gone out on this.

The weather that created difficulties for the Garda investigation paradoxically provided them with an advantage. The gales meant that the arsonists could not have sailed in to Tory, set the fire and left again. The arsonists were almost certainly still on the island. For the same reason that Gardaí had difficulties getting to the island, the arsonists could not have left it.

Some six weeks after the fire, islanders report that a lone Garda ventured out to Tory. He came on the morning ferry, spoke to a few islanders, and headed back to the mainland on the afternoon boat. None saw him make any forensic examination of the site. And any written record he made of his investigation has been lost, even to his very name.

While the Gardaí were not investigating the fire, the walls of Neville's house came tumbling down. These walls were three feet thick, built to defy the battering of Atlantic gales. The lime mortar that held the stones of the walls together was strong. For a while in the mid-1950s there had been no roof on the house, but those walls had stood firm. This did not happen in 1993. By March, large chunks had collapsed onto the road.

Patrick seemed to be taking the very existence of the ruins of Neville's house as an affront. In May 1993 Patrick's solicitor, John I Cannon, wrote to the Council regarding "Dangerous building on Tory Island" – "which said building is located at or near the proposed development site of the Hotel on Tory Island. Please note that my clients (Patrick and his hotel) intend to seek a demolition order on said building and please arrange to have said building inspected forthwith."

The house that disappeared on Tory Island

Patrick deployed a political canon as well. Minister of State for the Gaeltacht Pat 'The Cope' Gallagher wrote to the Council: "I make representations on behalf of Pat Doohan, Tory Island, Via. Letterkenny regarding the demolition of the old house in Tory and I would appreciate if you might let me know the up to date position regarding same." Patrick took an all-party approach; the Council also has a note of a phone call from Fine Gael TD, Dinny McGinley, complaining about the condition of the house.

On the 17th May 1993, the Council issued a notice through its solicitors: "Please note my clients (i.e. the Council) intend to seek a demolition order on said building and have it demolished forthwith." This never reached Neville. On the 16th June, Fr O'Neill rang the Council to report the house had fallen onto the road. By October 1993, the gables were all that remained of Neville's house.

At the end of the month, Council engineer Charlie Cannon visited Tory. He found the house damaged beyond repair. Charlie Cannon inspected the remains of the house and reported: "no works could be carried out to make this building safe without demolition." The report was as explicit as libel laws allowed. Charlie Cannon noted the house was:

"situated directly on the seaward side of the new Tory Island Hotel", and remarked: "How this building got into its present dangerous condition in such a short period of time (i.e. since work commenced on the New Hotel whose view it was blocking) is anybody's guess." None of the Council's senior officials thought Charlie Cannon's report worthy of investigation.

In January 1994, the Council acted at last. Charlie Cannon sent a fax to Patrick: "Dear Pat, As per our telephone conversation of earlier today, I would be obliged if you would clear the blocked County Road on Tory Island as soon as possible using the excavator which you have available on site, all I want done is the road made passable, which would mean pushing the stones debris (sic) into the side where the existing derelict building is. You can forward your bill to the above address for payment."

At the end of April 1994, a message from the Council finally reached Neville in New Zealand. By then, the house had vanished. An official with an illegible squiggle of a signature sent him a letter at his New Zealand address, headed "Dangerous Building at Tory Island" – "It has been brought to our attention that a building owned by you on Tory Island is in a dangerous condition. There is a new Hotel being built adjacent to this building and the owners are concerned that same will be a danger to the public as well as being unsightly (see attached photograph). Under the Derelict Sites Act, 1990, Donegal County Council are required to take whatever action is necessary to render this building safe. Storm damage has taken its toll on this building and considerable damage has been caused. I would be grateful if you could let us know what your intentions are regarding this property, before we proceed to enter the same on the Register of Derelict Sites."

The attached photo was blurred. There was no indication as to when it was taken. This was the Council's sole contact with Neville. Contrary to the legislation, he was served with no formal notice of his house being entered in the Register of Derelict Sites; nor served with a notice of measures he was to comply with to make the house safe.

While the destruction was occurring, Patrick owned the only digger on Tory. McGinty spent much of 1993 working on the island. 'Every time I went past, there was another bit (of the house) gone,' he said.

All this damage was done to the lower part of the house, within reach of the arm of the digger. During the High Court hearing, McGinty gave evidence of seeing Patrick's digger strike the house as it went past; he qualified this by adding he believed the collision was accidental.

The structural engineer's report, commissioned by Neville in 1994, determined the wall had received many other blows from a digger. Working from photographs, engineer Albert Fry concluded that only blows from machinery could have achieved the destruction of Neville's house. Fry ruled out wind as a cause: "We would point out that two of the walls remaining in vertical alignment i.e. the two gable walls, being the highest, would, in any storm, be subjected to the greatest wind forces. The clear defined lines of the remaining structure, being the gable walls and the remaining internal crosswall, would indicate that some form of mechanical plant has struck the building between these walls and parallel to them."

At some time between February 1993 and the start of the following year, the septic tank serving Neville's house was dug out, and replaced by the septic tank to serve Ostán Thoraigh. Neville's septic tank was sited on what had formerly been common land beside his house. In 1965 the previous owners had installed the tank. Over nearly 30 years, they and then Neville had acquired ownership by adverse possession, colloquially called "squatter's rights".

No witnesses came forward to say they had seen all this destruction. Neville's house was very visible. It was beside the road in Baile Thiar (West Town), the larger of Tory's two villages.

It would be easy to criticize islanders for not giving evidence. But Patrick was the richest and most powerful man on the island. He appeared to have the ear of the Council, Údaras na Gaeltachta (the authority for Gaeltacht areas) and local politicians. While there is no evidence that Patrick ever physically intimidated anybody, it was reasonable for islanders to assume that, if they spoke out, life could become awkward for them living, as they did, in a small isolated community. The Gardai and the Council had, by their inaction, shown they had no interest in investigating the destruction of the house. Any islander who gave evidence to the authorities might reasonably conclude they would get the same level of 'non-protection'. Patrick lived on the island, and islanders encountered him every day. Neville, on the other hand, was on the far side of the world. In the circumstances, it is understandable why the islanders claimed to have seen nothing.

Thus Neville's house cast no shadow over the official opening of Patrick's Ostán Thoraigh on May 11th 1994. Former island priest Fr Diarmuid Ó Peicín performed the blessing, and used the occasion to renew the dedication of Tory to the Sacred Heart. Fr Ó Peicín said he had noticed people with tears in their eyes during the blessing "as if the occasion was almost too much."

In retrospect, parts of the speech of Bord Fáilte Chief Executive Matt McNulty could have been phrased more appropriately: "… if more people took initiatives like Mr Doohan, a lot could happen." John Craig of the International Fund for Ireland (IFI), was not quite as unfortunate in his choice of words: "The project conformed to the IFI's primary objectives, the promotion of economic and social advance."

Minister of State Pat 'The Cope' Gallagher expressed the hope thousands would stay in Ostán Thoraigh. ABC television from America filmed the occasion, and interviewed Patrick. The local press reported: "The restaurant overlooks the harbour and back across Tory Sound to the mainland. From the dining room, guests had a panoramic sea view."

The house that disappeared on Tory Island

Chapter Three

The island from which Neville's house disappeared is the most remote inhabited outpost of the Celtic world. Eight miles north of the Donegal coast, Tory is sometimes referred to as 'Creag i lár na Farraige' – 'a rock in the middle of the sea'.

Tory is about three miles long, but so narrow that in places it is only a couple of hundred yards wide; its total area is 819 acres, the size of a large farm. It slopes downward from the north to the south; the northern side is cliffs, rising to a high point at the east end of the island.

The island has been inhabited for well over 2,000 years, starting with the early peoples who lived in Ireland. The most famous islander of pre-Christian times was the one-eyed giant Balor. Balor was a pirate, preying on passing shipping and mainland communities. Prehistoric ruins on the island's highest point are reputed to be the remains of his fort.

Saint Colmcille established a monastery here in the sixth century; it lasted a millennium until destroyed by English soldiers in 1595. The unusual Tau Cross that overlooks the island's pier was carved from a single piece of slate and dates from Colmcille's era.

The relative remoteness of Tory gave its inhabitants certain advantages. The sea was a defence against the wars, famines and diseases that ravaged the mainland. It was a defence, too, against landlords. They could not impose the same grip on Tory as they could on the mainland; collection of rents could vary from difficult to impossible. It protected the lucrative poitín distilling industry from the activities of excisemen.

The islanders could fish as well as farm, with plentiful seaweed to use for fertilizer. They lived on a busy sea route. For hundreds of years, until well into the twentieth century, there were scores of the small cargo boats that served Irish coastal ports passing the island. The sea was busy with fishing boats. Tory was the last piece of land passed by vessels bound for America, and the first met by those coming from the

New World. Especially in the days of sail, islanders used to sell or barter supplies to the many varieties of passing vessels. Sometimes the misfortunes of those vessels sent useful wrack onto the shores.

Until the outbreak of World War One in 1914, the weekly boat from Westport, County Mayo, to Glasgow, called in at certain times of the year. But first the disappearance of sailing boats in the early twentieth century, and then the decline in sea transport in the second half of the century, left Tory more isolated than it had been for centuries.

The island's population was concentrated in two villages; the larger An Baile Thiar (West Town) and An Baile Thoir (East Town). The population had gone above 400 in the nineteenth century. Over the next century or so, it fell to round 300. An unpublished official report in the 1970s recommended evacuating the population and making Tory either a prison or an artillery range for the Irish army. Given that level of official contempt, it is understandable there was an exodus of about half the population in the early 1980s. It seemed Tory would join the list of abandoned Irish islands. But the community showed resilience. The island priest called a meeting where the remaining islanders voted to stay; a campaign was started to improve facilities.

Round the time Neville's house disappeared, the population had hit its lowest point in recent history reaching approximately 120. Only 44 of 81 houses were permanently lived in. Young people, especially young women, had gone. There was no secondary school; many left at 13 to complete their education and did not return.

Fishing and farming were in decline. The arable land was partly exhausted due to centuries of use. Fishing was being squeezed by declining stocks; supertrawlers that hoovered up all fish life; EU restrictions; and a rational reluctance to face hardships and dangers for a small enough reward. The turf used for fuel that had been on the island had been dug out. The pier at An Baile Thiar that had been built in the early 20th century was not sheltered, making it impossible for boats to land in stormy weather.

Until a couple of years before the events of this book, there was no ferry to the island. The only regular communication was by the mail boat that sailed a couple of times a week from the mainland. Then Údarás na Gaeltachta (the authority for Gaeltacht areas) began a winter helicopter service in the mid-1980s.

Paradoxically, Tory's relative isolation was important in keeping people on the island. Those islands off Donegal which were closer to the coast were abandoned by the late 1970s. From them, the people could go to the mainland nearly every day. They could look out their windows and see the modern amenities they were missing. For the Tory people it was a major task to go to the mainland even in good weather; and in bad weather it was nigh impossible for weeks on end. Many islanders used to leave Tory only on rare occasions.

Tory's distance from the mainland meant that the islanders had to have a wide range of skills. They could build boats and houses, fix engines and machinery. What skills they lacked they had to develop – sometimes fast.

Tory was quite self-contained. It even kept the tradition of having a king. In the old days, he had overseen the allocation of strips of arable land to the islanders under a system similar to rundale; he made sure customs were maintained; and, being a literate person, was the accepted channel for communication with the authorities. A king still exists, but the title is more ceremonial. However, as is normal in such situations, there is a significant party seeking a more republican regime; and a minority who mutter about the need for regicide.

As with any small community, Tory has always had its internal tension but its relative isolation has meant people always had to depend on each other. Disagreements rarely came to blows because the survival of the community depended on avoiding serious splits. Sometimes tempers became frayed in drink but the next day the participants would be sure to see one another and make up.

In the early 1990s, life on the island was very restricted. Many of the conveniences of modern life, that were taken for granted on the mainland, were not available on Tory. There was just one shop with a limited stock. A trip to the supermarket was an expedition that had to be organized well in advance. The island was peaceful but with that came a feeling of emptiness because there were few people around. The number of visitors was small. The only vehicles were a few tractors and one old car. Many houses lay empty. Some were falling into a state of dereliction whilst others were occupied for only a couple of months in summer.

Two important facilities had been added over the previous years. The Comharchumann had opened a social club, which provided islanders with the luxury of draught Guinness; they had previously been restricted to bottles and cans. And there was a small chip shop, where the speciality was fresh deep-fried ling. Yet, for all its remoteness, the Tory of the early 1990s was part of a developed country. There was an electricity supply, and nearly every house had a deep freeze.

Irish was the language of everyday life. Tory was one of the strongest Irish-speaking areas in the country. The islanders had customized Irish to deal with the tasks of modern life. This produced words and phrases that were not for purists, such as the phrase 'ringeáil back' used about phone calls.

The islanders had kept many traditions and superstitions alive. Some of these had once been common on the mainland but had died out there; some were home grown. Many of them had been passed down from pre-Christian times. For example, the island's cursing stone is still buried somewhere in the old graveyard: by turning it and performing a ritual walk round the island, islanders believed they could draw down misfortune on their enemies. Up to the time Neville's house was destroyed, some islanders still felt there were other gods who could be called upon if the "God from the Chapel" failed to deliver.

Tory is a musical island. On the Donegal mainland the big instrument in traditional music has been the fiddle. Tory's big instrument was the accordion. This was because an accordion did not need to be re-tuned for months, whereas, if a string on a fiddle broke, a replacement could not easily be got on an island. There was a big store of traditional song on

Tory also. But the concept of sitting still in chairs listening to a concert was alien to the islanders. Music was something to be danced to; to which it was, often. The islanders had many dances of their own, practised at regular céilís.

What made Tory unique was the presence of a school of painters who were islanders. The tradition of painting began in the 1950s. An older islander met a visiting artist and expressed an interest in painting; the artist encouraged him. Then others followed the example. These Tory artists painted the world they knew. They developed a primitive style that was original. It did not follow traditional rules of proportion and perspective. Arguably, by breaking the rules, they were better able to depict the isolation, barrenness and savage seas of their island home. Importantly, painting has enabled a number of islanders to earn a living on Tory. Tory painters have held regular exhibitions. Some have shown significant imaginative powers, though none has ever depicted anything as bizarre as the disappearance of Neville's house.

Chapter Four

The two protagonists in the story of the house came from different backgrounds, but both had shown themselves to be strong-willed and determined. Neville was a son of the manse, university educated, romantic, creative, well-travelled and capable of both deep thought and impetuous action. Patrick had been born and reared in the small society of Tory and was a self-made man, who had pulled himself up to being the richest and most powerful man on the island by his mid-30s.

Neville's ancestors were Hugenots (French Protestants). The Précieux family were silk-weavers in La Rochelle on the west coast of France. When in 1685 the Catholic French king unleashed persecution on Protestants, the family Précieux fled for their lives and found refuge in Ireland. There they settled in the Lagan Valley west of Belfast, changed their skill to linen weaving, and their surname to Presho.

In 1947, nine generations later, Neville was born in Glasgow. His brother, Ian, followed in 1951. Their father had moved to Scotland to serve as a minister. In 1958 the Preshos returned to Ireland and settled in Holywood, Co. Down, a few miles east of Belfast.

The visual arts were always part of Neville's life. His maternal uncle, Robert Cochrane, was a photographer and a painter in watercolours. He was a strong presence in his nephew's life. When Neville was about seven or eight, it came naturally to him to start taking photographs with a small brownie camera. He recorded everything that was happening around him and kept the images.

Uncle Robert was creative on a number of fronts, regularly making model boats – complete with sails and rigging. Shortly after Neville started taking photographs, Uncle Robert enlisted him as a helper in the building of a proper rowing boat. Neville was the gofer, sent up to the shop for screws or whatever else was needed. He also watched what was done, and absorbed the information.

Like many Northern families, the Preshos had an affinity with Donegal. Family holidays were taken there. As Neville grew older, he would go on his own. He struck up friendships with local people in the Rosses, and sometimes went out fishing with them.

Neville spent the seven years of his secondary education at Sullivan Upper Grammar School in Holywood. The Sullivan of that time placed an emphasis on academic achievement. The sciences were stressed. Such 'fripperies' as art and music were taught for the first three years, but then pushed to one side in favour of the 'real' subjects needed for success in the professions. There were, however, significant liberal aspects about Sullivan. For example, the school had an Irish-language motto – unique for what was considered a Protestant school – "Lámh Foisdineach An Uachtar" (With the Gentle Hand Foremost)

Neville was one of the quieter and more reserved pupils in his class. He was not part of any group. He was very much his own man, making up his own mind about things, living life as he wished without being influenced by individuals or fashions. He was not chatty – but when he spoke, what he said counted. His sense of humour was very dry, stemming from an alternative view of the world. The general perception was that he was slightly eccentric – but no more than several others. He was one of those pleasant, easygoing pupils that classmates who may not have considered him a friend liked as a person.

Neville's contemporaries had the impression that he was always thinking about something – but not expressing it. Their impression was right. His creativity was bubbling away, though never manifested by taking part in school plays or concerts. Right through his school years he continued to take photographs. When he was seventeen he decided to follow Uncle Robert's example and build a ten-foot wooden boat – in the attic. That took two months, working on summer evenings with the sun streaming through the window. He kept the boat, until it was reduced to ashes in the fire on Tory Island.

In 1967 he passed A-Levels in Physics, Chemistry and Maths. He found Maths a struggle, but needed the subject for his chosen career path. That career was engineering. He had a dream of working on building a dam in Africa, and used to imagine himself looking down on his work in the African sunset.

He studied at Queen's University Belfast from 1967 to 1971. The rebellious spirit of the late 60s, social and political, had reached Belfast. Then the

Troubles began. All these upheavals barely touched him. Neville spent his days in the lecture theatres of the engineering faculty, and his evenings crouched over textbooks in the university library. A social life did not exist.

If life was dull during the academic year, Neville made up for it during the summer break. When Queen's broke up, his contemporaries headed for the building sites of London, the vegetable-canning factories of East Anglia, or the bars and hotels of Irish holiday resorts to find summer work. Neville, however, spent his first two summers working in Norway; during the second, he worked on the building of a dam. That job finished, he hitchhiked to the north of Norway and spent a couple of weeks with the indigenous Sami people. His third summer was spent in British Columbia on the west coast of Canada; and the summer he graduated was spent fishing for salmon in Alaska – having hitchhiked across the North American continent from New York.

There was no big plan behind his moving to London after graduation. He saw a job advertisement from consulting engineers Binnie and Partners. He did the interview and got the job. The advantage was that now he would get paid for his wanderlust. In 1972 his job took to him Nepal for a year, designing rural water supply schemes.

Nepal was not all about engineering. Neville also climbed into the foothills of Everest with an Italian Army expedition and reached as far as a base camp. With climbing Everest not possible, he climbed Kala Patta. It was a hillock by Himalayan standards, at a mere 18,200 feet. Oxygen was so thin on the summit that the blackness of the sky stuck in Neville's memory.

That year in Nepal switched the path of Neville's life from engineering to filmmaking. He was far from being a movie buff. He was not even a regular cinema-goer. He could not even be bothered watching films on TV from the comfort of his settee, because they did not spark his interest.

In rural Nepal, Neville found himself a witness to ways of life that were disappearing. Over centuries expert craftsmen had honed the skill of fashioning exquisite pots for the collection of water. Neville realized that the piped water system he was building would end their craft forever.

He wanted to record this lifestyle before it vanished. Film appeared the most suitable medium. On a visit to a Buddhist monastery, he met a BBC film crew which was making a documentary. It was his first ever meeting with anyone who worked in film.

He asked the director: 'What is the best way to make a film?' The resulting lesson was short: 'The best way is to just go and write a book and make a film. Or make a film about something you know about, and like. Regardless, you would need five percent money, ten percent skill and eighty-five percent tenacity'.

Neville returned to London overland. En route, he hitched a lift through Afghanistan's Khyber Pass perched on top of a lorry beside a group of bearded tribesmen toting Lee Enfield rifles.

Once back in London, Neville worked according to the second and third parts of the director's advice. He had gone salmon fishing a few times with brothers Frank and Conal Duggan from Kincasslagh in the Rosses. That gave him a subject. The Rosses were special to him, as somewhere he had known since childhood. His Uncle Robert had painted there, and visited for years. So Neville mortgaged his flat, cashed in his insurance policies, and borrowed from family members. The £6,000 (approximately £75,000 in today's terms) enabled him to hire a crew and equipment. In 1974 he spent his two week summer holiday making a film.

Neville, crew and equipment all arrived in Kincasslagh. Neville had never handled a film camera, studied film, or read a book on the subject. His first question to the crew was: 'What do I do?' The crew told him, and he did as they suggested. They were relieved at their unusual experience; working with a director who asked for their advice, listened to it, and acted accordingly.

Enthusiasm drove him through that first film. His engineering background was crucial in this venture, as he explained: 'Making a film is very like an engineering project and involves the same complex logistics, the same progress from conception to completion. Someone comes with a problem and you have to go away and think of a design, then improve it, commission it and execute the project. With film you start with something to film and plan the filming – which involves balancing people and resources and many other factors – and then you edit it. Showing the film is the successful completion.' Those two weeks in Kincasslagh produced thousands of feet of film.

Neville returned to London to complete his three year contract with Binnie and Partners. His contract finished the following April, and on that day he left the job and engineering to become a full time filmmaker. As soon as he had the loose ends of his London life tied up, he moved to Dublin with tins of film that needed serious editing. Dublin was the destination of necessity, because only there could he get money to complete the film, and he intended to make the rest of his films in Ireland.

He stored the tins of film under his bed in the flat he rented. Raising the money to transform the contents of the tins into a presentable film was a long, hard road. Funders did not immediately flock to his aid, but the raw film was of such good quality that RTE and the Northern Ireland Arts Council provided finance. During that summer of 1975 he spent a week in Donegal shooting some necessary extra sequences. Then he set to editing down the film. The result was "Summer Silver, a day in the life of a salmon fishing community".

"Summer Silver" does not look like the work of a man who had never held a film camera. The structure is straightforward. It opens early in the morning, at sea aboard the Duggan's boat, the Janeeta. From there, the film takes the viewer through the events of the next 24 hours, on land and sea. That includes the messy task where the salmon are gutted.

At the end, there is a powerful scene that is not part of the sequence of the day's events. The scene is powerful because it is about how fragile life is in a fishing community. Crewman 'Patrick Pirate' talks to camera about how he was dragged overboard while shooting nets. He and the crew struggled to get him back on board; he thought he was lost until dragged onto the boat by the feet. The near-death experience has made him take a big decision: "I've given up the sea. I want my family to have a father." That Neville includes this scene shows his confidence as a filmmaker.

Television stations round the world broadcast 'Summer Silver'. The film won prizes at international festivals including Cork, Huy in Belgium and Cartagena in Spain. Neville felt he had to become a professional filmmaker. He wanted to commit himself to the art – though that meant jumping from a well-paid job to being frequently penniless.

He mostly worked making documentaries. His only feature film was titled "Desecration" – the plot of which bore an uncanny resemblance to the events that would overwhelm Neville years later.

At the time it was made, in 1981, it seemed a piece of whimsy. The film is about the richest man on a small Irish island who arranges the destruction of an old castle that is perceived to be blocking a possible mine.

"Desecration" is set on the fictional island of Inish na Ron (The Island of the Seals). Former teacher Muiris Conroy, an outsider, has retired to the island. He is restoring Inish na Ron's old castle, 'The Cashel', and seeking to have it declared a national monument. Then three geologists arrive, prospecting for tungsten – which they find under 'The Cashel' . This gives hope of development.

The great preacher of development is John Joe Hernon, Inish na Ron's publican and hotelier. Hernon incites a gang of drunken islanders to wreck 'The Cashel', telling them: "Who is Conroy to take over the Cashel anyway? Let him not interfere with the good of the island." Hernon is not present during the attack, but is in his kitchen drinking a glass of whiskey. There he tells his sister: "Do you know what I'm doing in the morning? I'm going to the mainland to get planning permission for an extension, and see about a grant." In the light of subsequent events, the plot does not seem so improbable.

However, it was Neville's consistent output of documentaries which built his reputation. So high was this that, in 1983, the Irish Film Board funded him to travel to America to study film distribution and the United Nations hired him to make a documentary on alternative technology.

Neville's film career ran parallel to a love affair with Tory. He first came on the island when out fishing with the Duggans in the early 1970s: 'We were loading the nets this morning, and the sun was rising, and I could see in front of me this delightful orangey-pink island. I said to Frank: "Where's that? I must go there."'

In July 1976 he made his first visit. He went out on a crowded half-decker from Magheroarty on the mainland. The boat docked at Port an Dúin on the east end of the island. His journey on to the Baile Thiar was completed on a trailer towed by a tractor. As it jolted down the hill into the Baile Thiar, Neville was struck by a strange smell, none too pleasant at first whiff. That smell was rotting sea-rods. Always after, he would associate that smell with his first experience of Tory. Helpful islanders sent him to the only B&B, where he promptly struck up a friendship with the owner.

Neville had chosen a key night in Tory's history to arrive, the night the Social Club was being opened. The Club was jam-packed. Neville still remembers the céilí as "mighty". The music and dancing finally petered out round five in the morning. He walked back to the B&B in bright daylight.

He stayed three or four days. During those days he fell in love with Tory. He had never been anywhere similar. It was a real living island. He spent his time walking round, and photographed as much as he could to make a record. People were working in the fields, stacking hay and tending crops. Twice a day cows were brought home from the fields for milking. The milk was churned into butter. Every house was baking bread. The only motorized transport was provided by a few tractors. They were pulling trailer-loads of hay along the road. Islanders were gathering sea-rods (a type of seaweed) from the shore. Boats were arriving at the harbour with turf for the winter, other boats were leaving taking cattle. It was a busy island, with a population of round 300. The only necessities that had to come from the mainland were turf, tobacco, whiskey and beer. The island's one road had not been tarred, so it was rough red granite.

Neville had embraced film because he wanted to record disappearing ways of life. In the few weeks after he returned to Dublin, he raised £6,000 (€7,620) to make a film that would do that for Tory; though he could not know how quickly the Tory of 1976 was going to disappear, its demise hastened by the exodus of the early 1980s . By August he had the funding to return to the island, with a film crew that was a mixture of professionals and friends. They made "Oileán/An Island".

The film is a tribute to the culture and way of life of Tory. "Oileán/An Island" recorded Tory as the bustling place it was in 1976. It showed the islanders as busy, hard-working, resourceful and content. There was little dialogue; Neville allowed the images to speak for themselves. That little dialogue was quietly spoken in Irish, about everyday things. There were just a short few sentences spoken in English at the very end, as a voice-over.

Similarly to "Summer Silver", the film showed a day in the life of a community; from the woman getting up in the morning and letting out the hens and ducks, to the community going en masse to the céilí in the Social Club at night. Neville got top Irish-language folk-rock group Clannad to provide the music. The teenage Patrick was one of the islanders most featured. In one scene, he was mowing oats with a scythe. In a longer sequence, he was loading lobster pots onto a cart; taking them to the pier; then unloading them onto the wall.

More than quarter of a century after the film was made, the then Gaeltacht minister Éamonn Ó Cuiv praised its importance: "Neville Presho's film 'Oileán' represents a fascinating look at life on Tory island, Co. Donegal during the 1970's... As Minister with responsibility for the inhabited offshore islands, I believe it is important to recognise that the islands represent a rich and vibrant element of our heritage.

This film provides a snapshot of an island community at a moment in time. Thanks to the work of the (Irish film) archive, this moment has been captured on film for future generations who may wish to look at the evolution of a Donegal island community."

After the summer of 1976, Tory became the place in Donegal to which Neville went for solace. Work as a filmmaker kept him Dublin-based. In those years, there was not a lot of money in Irish filmmaking but this was what he wanted to do. He spent most of his time raising finance bit by little bit from the various funders. Tory gave him a refuge from the non-stop pressure of making one project on a shoestring, while raising the money for the next, all the time under constant financial pressure. He went over to the island two or three times per year. In summer he would come up from Dublin for a few weeks, then take a few days here and there at other times of the year. The Tory people had liked the way they were portrayed in "Oileán/An Island". So when he went back, he was welcomed as a friend.

Neville made his love of Tory into a long-term commitment when, in 1982, he bought a house for £3,000(€3,810). That sum represented his life savings. The two-story house above the harbour was one of the few on the island looking south. There was a spectacular view of the coast, from Muckish mountain in the east to Arranmore Island in the west. It was an old house, not outstanding architecturally, but with character. The stone walls had been plastered and Neville whitewashed them every year. He did his best to upgrade the house, digging a drain round the outside walls and thus reducing the damp. The islanders were friendly to him, but he stayed an outsider. He never learned Irish. However, after a couple of years, he could understand what people were saying and had picked up a few phrases. Life for Neville was going well. But that was not to last.

Career-wise, he tried to expand as a filmmaker and, in 1986, he put together a proposal to buy a film studio, enlisting a Hollywood major in the project. He was knocking on the door of the big time, and it was opening. Then it slammed in his face and he tumbled back down the steps to the bottom. He received a letter saying the major's parent company had decided to pull out of Europe – and the deal was cancelled.

Neville had over-extended himself financially to put the deal together, and was left catastrophically exposed. He was broke, burdened with debt, and had no chance of being able to finance a film in Ireland. Additionally, he was suffering the psychological wear and tear of a dozen years of filmmaking.

The House that disappeared on Tory Island

This personal catastrophe happened at the worst of times, because Ireland was in deep recession. Unemployment was running at 17%. Twenty-eight thousand emigrated in 1986. In October, Neville became one of them.

Before leaving, he bought a load of oak planks, loaded them into his car and headed for Donegal. It was a time when the Gardaí were on alert. Neville was stopped and searched twice on his way to the mail boat at Bunbeg by Gardaí suspecting that the driver of a heavily-laden Northern-registered car might be carrying a load of explosives. On Tory, he spent the best part of a week boarding up every window in his house. He gave a key to an older island woman who had become a friend, and left an address and phone number for his parents.

Neville had no worries about leaving the house unattended. There was no vandalism on Tory. It was a waste of money to pay insurance on a house there, because arson was unheard of. That sort of thing happened in the troubled North, not on idyllic Tory.

The House that disappeared on Tory Island

Chapter Five

The first stop for the emigrant Neville was Australia, on a visitor's visa. Once there he got a job working for AAISH, a charity for the learning disabled. His new employers put him in charge of giving vocational training to twenty intellectually disabled adults on a farm in the outer suburbs of Sydney. Manager R Howell's testimonial is evidence of Neville's capabilities before illness took over:

"In his work Mr Presho's attention to detail and sound commonsense have enabled me to rely on him for the best possible results to flow. His good humour and seemingly endless patience has meant that in perhaps the most difficult field of work, even some of the more onerous duties associated with intellectually disabled people have been attended to without hesitation."

After nine months Neville's visa ran out so he moved on to New Zealand where he hoped there would be openings in filmmaking. His skills were known there because New Zealand television had screened five of his films. He flew in to Auckland and went to the headquarters of New Zealand Television. The interviewer was sympathetic, but had no job for him. He suggested Neville try the wildlife part of the service. This was based 900 miles away in Dunedin, at the other end of the country towards the bottom of the South Island. Neville hitched the journey non-stop. The interviewer there was impressed with his work – but not enough to give him a job.

Neville had changed hemispheres, while keeping his penchant for remote islands. Before landing at Auckland Airport he had never heard of Stewart Island. On his way to Dunedin, one of the drivers who gave him a lift told him about it. Neville remembers nothing of that driver, not the face, not even if the person was man or woman – just that the driver had told him about Stewart Island. Once he heard of the island, he knew that was where he wanted to go.

When the New Zealand Television asked him for a forwarding address, he gave the Post Office on Stewart Island – without even knowing such a place existed. Two and a half days after arriving in Auckland, he stepped off the ferry onto Stewart Island. That would be home for the next two years.

Stewart Island is the most southerly inhabited part of New Zealand, nineteen miles south of the South Island. The next land was Antarctica. Stewart Island was 300 times the area of Tory – with only about three times the population. Neville first became a cray fisherman, then a labourer on the installation of a power scheme. The work was wet, cold and muddy – but he adapted to it. After a year he started working on some possible screenplays. He put together a proposal for a film called 'Islands of the Glowing Skies'. It was about two fishermen who meet, one from Tory and the other from Stewart Island.

He went to London to raise the cash, but funders were not interested. One evening, he called in to a pub in the Archway for a drink – and bumped into Patrick. Each was very pleased to meet a friendly face in a foreign city, and they shared a very pleasant few drinks.

After Neville had been a couple of years on Stewart Island, a friend invited him up to Queenstown in the interior of the South Island. Queenstown is a centre for skiing and adventure tourism. It lies in a beautiful situation on a lake, surrounded by mountains. It was peaceful, being a hundred miles from the nearest city, Invercargill. Neville got casual manual work; mostly landscaping gardens or painting houses. He used his photography skills, producing a poster showing views of the Queenstown area. Also when in

Queenstown, Neville joined the New Life Church. This was a Pentecostal Church to which a friend had introduced him. The New Life Church was different to anything Neville had experienced. But he was open to new spiritual experiences.

A film career was not all Neville left behind in Ireland. In 1980 he had met Fiona, a Dublin woman and physiotherapist. As they walked through the Dublin mountains on one of their first dates, he realized this was the woman he wanted to marry. Settling down was difficult. He was frantically running about trying to get funding for a film project, sometimes striking lucky and then being engrossed in filming. Fiona was busy working, and forced to travel to Scotland, Norway, and various parts of Donegal to get employment.

After Neville emigrated they kept in touch by letter, at least once a week. They could also phone but this could be difficult as Neville usually had no phone in his accommodation. Neville liked to do some things in a traditional way. In 1989 he wrote to Fiona's father asking for his daughter's hand in marriage – and got a positive response. In 1990 he returned to Ireland and the couple married in a ceremony conducted by his father. The wedding was quiet, with just family and a few close friends. Then it was off to an island for their honeymoon; Inisheer, the smallest of the Aran Islands. Neville had also made a film there, "Obair an Lae" (The Day's Work). The honeymoon over, they returned to Queenstown where they settled in a one bedroom flat.

Life was financially precarious. The various manual jobs Neville was working at were not as prestigious as film making. They were almost as remunerative, though – and a good deal less stressful. Fiona stayed at home, while Neville went out to put food on the table. The couple soon had two children, first David, then Rachel. So they lived in frugal comfort until April 1994. As autumn moved toward winter, Neville received Donegal County Council's letter saying his house was in a dangerous condition.

That was an unpleasant surprise, but did not seem a disaster. Neville could not work out what the Council's concern was about. The letter gave him the impression the house had been badly damaged by some weather event. He did not want his house knocked down. He talked things over with Fiona. They decided to return to Ireland for the first time in four years. Money was short, and Neville's father helped with their fare. Events when he returned to Ireland would change his life forever, and for the worse.

* * *

The other main participant in the ensuing events was Patrick. Patrick was single-minded. His life until 2009 had been less varied than Neville's but with more stable financial success. Patrick was born September 1958. The Doohans were one of oldest families on Tory, rooted on the island for over half a millennium. They lived in the Baile Thoir. The smaller Baile Thoir saw itself as the real, traditional Tory, in contrast to the cosmopolitan melting pot that was the larger Baile Thiar.

Patrick's family were known as 'Brianaigh' Doohans, from a forbearer named Brian, to separate them from others of the name on Tory. Some families in the Baile Thoir were noted for singing, or accordion playing, or dancing; the 'Brianaigh' Doohans were known for their hard work, on land and sea.

After primary school, Patrick went to secondary school on the mainland for a couple of years but his interests did not lie in studying. He left school and established himself as a good fisherman of salmon, lobster, and a bit of herring. He was not gregarious, but had inherited the family dedication to hard work.

Tory in the 1970s was a narrow place for a young man. At round the age of twenty Patrick moved to London. At the time there was a sizeable community of Tory exiles in the English capital. London widened his horizons in various ways. Patrick became a joiner, working at shuttering for concrete. He tried his hand at amateur boxing but proved to be more successful at martial arts, achieving a black belt.

Patrick had the hard-headed determination to thrive, if modestly, in London. He maintained the Doohan family's dedication to working hard. Where other Irishmen drank their wages after knocking off work, Patrick took a second job at night, as a bouncer in Irish entertainment venues.

He married another Irish emigrant, Bernie from Co Mayo, started a family, and bought a substantial house. He got the money together to buy a second house, and became a landlord to other Irish immigrants. The accommodation he provided was not luxurious, but he could show generosity. Several tenants who ran out of money were told they could pay their rent whenever they got some money together.

Patrick spent approximately fifteen years in England. By then the Irish economy was powering out of a long recession. With Irish property prices still lower than London's, returning emigrants who had sold up could come home with substantial funds. And, with the Irish economy taking off, a hard-working tradesman could make the jump up in class into becoming a businessman. Patrick became one of the cubs of the Celtic Tiger. Soon he would have his own business.

In 1989 the Comharchumann had drawn up a development action plan for Tory. This suggested rebuilding Wards at a cost of £60,000 (E76,200), as a key facility for visitors and islanders; the restored building would include a library and museum, with bedrooms upstairs for visitors. The Comharchumann was still mulling over these plans when Patrick swept back on to Tory. He had grander ideas, proposing a hotel and convincing the committee it was what Tory needed. To many islanders, here was a man who had succeeded in the outside world. His plans swayed the Comharchumann committee to drop the previous plan, and sell Wards to him.

State agencies backed Doohan and Ostán Thoraigh. Údarás na Gaeltachta bought €126,974 worth of shares, and approved grants of €59,043. The hotel attracted widespread publicity because of its unusual location. Another man held the title of King of Tory but Patrick was the real monarch of the island.

Chapter Six

After Neville discovered his house on Tory had been destroyed, it seemed a malevolent spirit stalked the Preshos to the other side of the world. Their life in New Zealand tumbled into a nightmare. Mr Justice Murphy summed up some of that nightmare in the High Court in 2009:—"Between 1994 and 2000, the Plaintiff (Neville) suffered from mental instability, repeated hospitalisation, detention, and ongoing medication and alcohol dependency."

The patient and good humoured Neville who had lived for 46 years was no more. The old Neville had been a social drinker, who enjoyed a glass of wine or a pint of beer when in company. As the 90s progressed, he lost control of his drinking. Friends were shocked at the way he would down a bottle of wine where before he had sipped at a couple of glasses. All his life he had been a peaceful, law-abiding citizen. In drink, he had some minor but distressing encounters with the New Zealand police. For years, he had been a moderate smoker who stopped smoking from time to time. The new Neville was a chain smoker, puffing cigarette after cigarette.

Neville's concentration became poorer and poorer. This left him increasingly unable to work for any length of time. He was a proud man, reluctant to apply for benefits. Fiona was looking after the children, so not working outside the home. As a result the Preshos were "living on the bones of their arse" to quote the popular New Zealand expression. They survived for a period on milk and potatoes which a sympathetic neighbour left at the back door of their flat.

As a member of the Queenstown New Life Church, Neville believed he had a duty to God to forgive those he considered had wronged him, and to get on with his life. For months at a time he embraced forgiveness but the memory of what had happened to his house was eating away at him. Every few months it came back to the surface to cause him distress. That in turn threw him into a deep depression. Each of those deep depressions sent Neville further into a downward spiral, becoming more and more obsessed with the house in Tory. He struggled on with whatever work he could get. His final job, as a projectionist in Queenstown's cinema, lasted for a year.

The stresses of Neville's illness, small children, and poverty, were catastrophic for Fiona. She was a non-smoker, had normal blood pressure, and was the correct weight for her build. Despite this, she suffered two strokes and four miscarriages. The second stroke nearly killed her; she had to be taken to hospital by helicopter. After her recovery, symptoms she developed led doctors to suspect she had developed multiple sclerosis. Just for once, the Preshos had some luck: Fiona did not have multiple sclerosis. But because of her health, Neville had to give up his job as projectionist to look after the children. He was never to work again.

The hell that had invaded Neville and Fiona's lives blighted the lives of their children as well. The eldest child broke his leg three times in the same place as a result of osteogenesis imperfecta (a genetic condition that caused brittle bones). Further tests showed he had Aspergers syndrome. In the late 90s, the couple had two more children, a boy and a girl, who were also caught up in their parents' misfortunes. Because of Neville and Fiona's ill health, friends had to look after the children from time to time. However, during a couple of particularly severe parental illnesses, all the children were taken into care.

On 13th September 1999, the Preshos' life hit its lowest point. In the morning, Neville's father rang with the sad news that Neville's brother Ian had died of double pneumonia. It was difficult to come to terms with this. Then, less than twelve hours later, Fiona's mother rang to inform them that Fiona's father had died. The awfulness overwhelmed them. They were on the other side of the world, suffering recurrent ill-health, with no chance of attending either of the funerals, unable to be there with their families – or get emotional support from them.

The next day Fiona was in physical agony and had to be taken to hospital. About a week later the pressure of these new misfortunes overwhelmed Neville, and he had to be admitted to a psychiatric hospital. The children were taken into care.

It was almost Christmas when Fiona and Neville were discharged from their respective hospitals. Social Services asked to meet them. At the meeting they found that, confused and ill, they had signed over care of their children on a permanent basis. After negotiations, which included their solicitor, they were allowed to take their children back on condition they return to Ireland and live with Neville's parents. Ian had left the family some money in his will. Friends encouraged them to return to Ireland and make a new start.

Neville was not keen to return to Ireland, though he was the only one of the family who was not a New Zealand citizen. A few days before the flight he took an overdose of medication. He was still recovering when Fiona got him onto the plane.

The Neville who moved back was unrecognisable from the driven filmmaker who had left fourteen years previously. He had declined physically and his strength had gone. In April 2000, they moved in to live with Neville's elderly parents in Holywood. After a while, they were able to raise the money from various sources to buy a house. But there was no new start, only the same misery in a different country. Neville has not been able to work since his return from New Zealand. He has no mental stamina, certainly not enough for day's work.

Fiona encouraged him to seek some sort of redress for the disappearance of the house, in the hope it would bring him closure. Thus, the year after he returned, Neville decided to apply for planning permission to build a two-storey house on the site on Tory. He erected a site notice which, according to islanders, disappeared soon after he returned to the mainland. His mind was in turmoil, and he did not proceed to lodging a planning application with the Council.

In the first week of October 2001, Neville returned again to Tory. He had a few drinks in the hotel bar, then walked over to Dún Bhaloir (Balor's Fort), the highest point on the island. There he took off all his clothes, and laid an oilskin coat that he had brought back from New Zealand on the ground. He lay naked on it all night as he prayed that God would grant the island forgiveness. Next morning he put his clothes on, descended from the Fort, wrote a document, and asked the secretary in the Comharchumann offices to type it for him.

Then he sought out Patrick in Ostán Thoraigh, and the two signed the document which was witnessed by the Comharchumann secretary:

"We the undersigned Neville Presho and P Doohan do this day 2001 enter into a binding agreement, where I P Doohan will secure the land rights to the area shown shaded, for Neville Presho, and will assign to him the land rights and ownership of that area. In pursuance, I Neville Presho, will simultaneously assign the land rights and ownership of the land known as folio 13745F in O.S. 6 Co Donegal to Patrick Joseph Doohan of Ostán Thoraigh. This is a straight swap transaction and does not involve any fanancial (sic) remuneration to either party." The document was accompanied by a sketch of a possible site on the island which was also signed and witnessed.

Then Patrick signed a document that supported Neville's grandiose plans for a Tory Visitor Centre. It said: "Neville's ideas and enthusiasm will ensure that

Tory becomes a major tourist attraction in Ireland." With his documents signed, Neville took the ferry back to the mainland. Two days later he was admitted to a psychiatric hospital in Downpatrick.

Neville never got his site on Tory. Giving evidence in the High Court, Patrick said he had never intended to implement the agreement as it was not realistic.

On the other hand, Patrick was still capable of acts of kindness. During one of his visits to Tory, Neville ran out of money. Patrick loaned him €100.

Chapter 7

Neville was obsessed with the loss of the house. He had been violated. One of the things he cherished most dearly had been taken from him and destroyed. Worse, he felt powerless to do anything about it. That experience of powerlessness worsened his illness. In turn, illness made it more difficult for him to properly explain the origin of his woes. That led him into further stress. To assist in making a new planning application to build on the former site of his house, he retained a solicitor. Soon their relations broke down irretrievably. The solicitor wrote to him:

"We confirm that we are no longer willing to represent you in this or any other matter. We await receipt of Authority from another Solicitor in order that we may release your file. No fee note will be raised. We request that you do not contact this office."

A few months after the family's return from New Zealand, Neville contacted Donegal County Council seeking copies of all its reports on the matter. The Council provided these. Even with this documentation, Neville could find no way to move his case forward. Thus the wrong festered, until one morning Neville's life intersected with mine.

From the mid-90s to the mid noughties, I was a regular visitor to Tory. There I heard of the wrong done to Neville. Several islanders were unhappy at the injustice and told me of the events. I had found the story of the house fascinating – but I had no way to contact its owner. It seemed that, almost certainly, I would never be able to properly establish what happened. Then a coincidence like an unlikely plot twist from a TV soap threw Neville and me together.

At Easter 2003 he, Fiona, and their children were staying in Bunbeg on the Donegal mainland. On Easter Saturday they decided to go out to Tory for the day. It was a perfect, calm, sunny day in April, like that nine years before when Neville had travelled over on the same ferry to discover his house had disappeared.

I was on the ferry that morning, going over to Tory until the next day. Neville stood in the prow, as he had done nine years before. He saw me, decided I looked an interesting person (he has never explained whether he meant this as a compliment or not), and

Neville Presho

Patrick Doohan

An Baile Thiar, 1982, from sea

Neville's House

Ward's Hotel mid-1980s

The Street, Baile Thiar

Ruins of house and hotel

Hotel overlooking site of house

moved over to strike up a conversation. To me, this tall, bearded vigorous man of around fifty seemed very pleasant. Then, after a couple of minutes, I realised this was the man whose house had vanished. I tentatively raised the subject with Neville. When he responded, I was able to give him some more information. When Neville pushed me further, I explained to him that I could not name my sources because of journalistic privilege.

Neville cooled towards me. He had finally found a man who knew things that he was desperate to know, but who would only give him limited information. I would like to say that I immediately sprang to the alert on meeting him but I was off duty for the weekend. For a couple of days I was a holidaymaker on a short break, not a journalist. When the boat docked in the harbour, I let Neville walk off and we went our separate ways. And, although we met again a couple of times whilst on the island, we parted without my even getting his phone number. That night the Preshos returned to Bunbeg.

The following evening the ferry brought me back there. As I walked up from the harbour to my car, Neville and Fiona were sitting in front of their B&B. Fiona saw me first. When she pointed me out to Neville, he raced down the pier, stopped me, and said: 'Will you give me a name and phone number?'

The House that disappeared on Tory Island

A couple of nights after that exchange, I rang Neville. After a week or two, I suggested a solicitor to him; Michael Gillespie, a Glasgwegian living at the Braade, beside Carrickfin Airport in the Rosses. Gillespie was a stocky bald-headed Celtic supporter, who showed both toughness and stamina. He had run several marathons in under three hours. A karate expert, he had reached the finals of the Shukokai competition in Glasgow's Kevlin Hall a couple of times. His rough style did not go down well with referees, and he did not win any trophies.

Gillespie had spent over 20 years practising law in Glasgow. A lot of his work had been civil, on behalf of marginalised and disadvantaged individuals. He had taken negligence cases against other lawyers. He had obtained damages for the parents of a little girl who was fatally injured falling from a taxi on the M8 motorway. Her death was due to the absence of a simple plastic guard over the door handle. It could have been fitted at the cost of 50 pence per handle on older models of taxi, but Glasgow City Council's licensing authority had not bothered to require it.

As well as having a legal reputation, Gillespie had built up a certain cult following in the west of Scotland as guitarist, mandolin player and vocalist with folk-rock band Emerald Country. He specialized in Dubliners-type numbers, but could make the switch to rock or country mode when that was what the audience wanted. Emerald County had made it big on the island of Mull, where they regularly played the summer festival. Their appearance at Barrafest on the isle of Barra was their most spectacular performance. The marquee collapsed during their set.

In the late 1990s, with a young family, Gillespie decided to relocate to his parents' native West Donegal taking his guitar and mandolin with him. By this stage, he could sing a mean Bob Dylan. West Donegal was not as violent as Glasgow – though doing its best to catch up – but he found it more lawless.

In his few years in Donegal, Gillespie had built a reputation as the lawyer who would fight hard cases. On behalf of several dozen small landowners, he was fighting a long ongoing battle with Donegal International Airport and private developers regarding ownership of the airport site. His ambition was not to be part of the legal, political and business establishment, but rather to question it.

Gillespie did more than act as Neville's legal representative. He was angry at the injustice done to his client. Gillespie became more than a legal representative; he was a friend and confidant to Neville. One of the psychiatrists who treated Neville, Dr Clifford Haley, believed Gillespie's support was crucial to Neville's health withstanding the pressures of the trial.

As well as launching legal action, Gillespie helped Neville put pressure on the Gardaí. The two went to Sligo and met Assistant Commissioner Byrne. They sought to see the Garda files on the investigation into the fire. These were refused.

Where the meeting was most useful was that Byrne took time to talk to Neville. After the conversation, the Assistant Commissioner clearly appreciated the seriousness of what had happened. As a result, the Garda investigation recommenced. Detective Garda David Moore carried this out. Moore went to Tory in the autumn of 2003. There he spoke to many of the island's adult population. Patrick was the only person who made a statement. While rumours naming several suspects had been circulating since 1993, there was no evidence to bring charges.

Neville made a formal complaint to the Garda Complaints' Board regarding the conduct of the initial investigation in 1993-4. The complaint was deemed "inadmissible" because of the passage of time. However, by then senior Garda officers recognized there had not been a proper investigation in 1993-4. The force held an internal review into its failure and, though Neville and Gillespie were not allowed to see a copy, the review had an important outcome. As a result of its findings, the Gardaí agreed Superintendent Eugene McGovern would give evidence in court on behalf of Neville.

As these developments were taking place, the process of getting Neville's case to court was grinding on. In September 2003 Gillespie fired the first shot with a letter to Patrick. He gave the hotelier notice that Neville was seeking €250,000 in damages:-

"My client (Neville) has provided me with information to the effect that his dwellinghouse was destroyed and removed entirely from the ground by you and/or persons working on your behalf, and my client holds you liable for the very substantial loss, injury and damage which he has suffered as a result of this matter."

Gillespie further alleged the site of Neville's house was being used as a car park for the hotel:-

"If you continue to use my client's property for car parking purposes or otherwise trespass on his land, then proceedings for an injunction may issue against you without further warning. My client informs me that one of the septic tanks serving the hotel has been placed on his property and I require an undertaking from you within the next 14 days that this will be removed and that there will be no further interference with my client's property, failing which an injunction will be sought in this regard also."

Patrick's solicitor, John I Cannon, fired off a barrage of refutations on behalf of his client. Cannon denied Patrick had any connection to the demolition of Neville's house:- "My client has not interfered in any way whatsoever with whatever lands your client owns and which adjoins his property on the island. My client also denies that he erected a septic tank serving the hotel on your client's property. My client (Patrick) has been much offended by the allegations contained in your said letter and he would like to take this opportunity to impress upon your client that he should be careful in future as to what he alleges against my client. The allegations in your said letter are totally untrue and unfounded."

Over the next two years, both sides exchanged letters. Patrick and his legal team were slow in their replies.

Gillespie approached barrister Peter Nolan to represent Neville in the High Court. A judge once called Nolan an "old warhorse". Nolan is known as a fiercely effective cross-examiner, able to find any chink in an opposing witness' evidence and lever it open. Gillespie sent the papers in the case to Nolan towards the end of March 2004. Nolan initially thought they were an April Fool joke that had arrived early.

In January 2006, summonses were formally issued against Patrick, alleging destruction of the house and ongoing trespass. Patrick refused to accept them. Three months later, the High Court ordered that they be served 'by placing them in an envelope and putting it through the letter box at his residence.' The summons server delivered them into the letterbox of Patrick's home.

The claims in the summons were comprehensive. Neville sought:—

—Damages for trespass, interference with the Plaintiff's (Neville's) property and unlawful and continued unauthorised use of the Plantiff's property;

—An Order that the Defendants do restore the said lands to the Plaintiff, restore and rebuild a dwellinghouse on the said lands equivalent to (sic) in size and proportion to the dwellinghouse wrongfully and unlawfully demolished by the Defendant (Patrick);

—An order that the Defendants do remove the septic tank or tanks from the property of the Plaintiff placed there unlawfully, remove the car park, fencing, stones and boulders and all of the other objects placed unlawfully and without the consent of the Plaintiff on the Plaintiff's property;

—That if necessary any purported agreement as between the Plaintiff and the first named Defendant of and concerning the Plaintiff's property dated the 4th of October 2001 should be set aside and declared null and void;

—And asking such further and or other order that his Honourable Court deems appropriate.

This bombshell shook Patrick into action. Cannon fired off another barrage in which he again vehemently refuted every allegation Neville had made. He further denied Neville's septic tank had ever been installed beside the house. Cannon added a new missile; that the Statute of Limitations barred any legal action (after more than seven years) because "the claim as contended herein, or at all, was brought, after such a lengthy and inexcusable delay."

As the legal process crept towards the court hearing, Neville's health continued to decline. He was admitted twice to Downpatrick psychiatric hospital. Consultant psychiatrist Dr J Green described his condition as complex and challenging to manage: "He continues to experience subjective low mood, with feelings of unhappiness and fatigue. He finds himself having difficulty coping with the stresses of everyday life."

Under all the strain, Neville and Fiona's marriage broke up. Neville had to return to live with his elderly parents, while Fiona stayed in the marital home. Increasing his distress, there were repeated delays in getting a date for a High Court hearing. This was to be held in Letterkenny rather than the normal venue of Dublin. Because witnesses from Tory were being called, some elderly, Gillespie believed there was a better chance of their attending in Letterkenny. Matters were also slowed because the case was being held in Irish at Patrick's request. Thus all papers had to be translated for the benefit of the non-Irish speaking Gillespie and Nolan.

As the trial approached the two legal teams lined up. To work with Nolan, Gillespie hired Cormac Ó Dulacháin, an Irish-speaking senior counsel. Ó Dulacháin was shrewd and battle-hardened, with a perpetual smile – particularly broad when playing with hostile witnesses. Nolan and Ó Dulacháin had the same gifts: they were able to put clients at their ease, and never gave their clients false hopes.

Patrick's barrister was Séamas Ó Tuathail. In a previous life, Ó Tuathail had been a Republican internee in the North; and, in the late 60s and early 70s, editor of Republican newspaper *The United Irishman*. Through the paper, he had campaigned against ground rents and private ownership of fisheries. Accompanying Ó Tuathail would be two junior counsel, both Irish-speaking.

The House that disappeared on Tory Island

Mr Justice Roderick Murphy was listed to hear the case. Those who know Murphy describe him as "an assiduous worker, a good conversationalist and a gentleman." Sitting without a jury, the judgment would be his alone.

Chapter Eight

Neville's case finally came to hearing on 2nd March 2009 at the High Court, sitting in Letterkenny Courthouse with Mr Justice Murphy presiding. It proved to be three and a half days of classic courtroom drama.

Shortly before 11am on that Monday morning, Patrick made his entrance accompanied by his legal team. He was tall and confident in a light-coloured jacket, smiling in an affable way and exchanging a couple of good-humoured words with those he knew around the court – including the present writer. He looked every inch the Donegal man made good, in the full bloom of health and prosperity. But, as in all good dramas, there was a little sign that all was not well. Except for his legal team, Patrick seemed to be on his own. No group of islanders had come to support him.

The six years since I had met him on the ferry had been cruel to Neville. The previous week he had been discharged from yet another spell in a psychiatric hospital. The tall and vigorous man of 2003 had shrunk and had an air of frailty; he was now completely bald, and his skin pale.

The opening of this drama was low key. There were only two journalists at the press table, Áine Ní Bhreasláin from TG4 and myself. Áine had to leave the room from time to time to attend to other jobs.

Cormac Ó Dúlacháin outlined the destruction of the house and its replacement by the car park and septic tank. Séamas Ó Tuathail denied every allegation, accused Neville of making wild and untrue allegations about his client and others, and claimed the case should be disbarred by the statute of limitations as the events were agreed to have happened 16 years beforehand.

Then Neville provided the first touch of drama. In the witness box he told of approaching Tory fifteen years beforehand on the ferry, and his shock at seeing his house had disappeared. Several times he broke down in tears, going on to describe how the fall-out had destroyed his life. His voice failed into a whisper. He held the attention of the courtroom, every ear cocked to hear every word.

As the court adjourned at the end of the day, the Judge gave a broad hint that there should be a settlement. "The evidence given is quite dramatic," he said. "I would ask the parties to consider overnight." He reminded both parties of the 2001 agreement (whereby Patrick agreed to give Neville a site on Tory) and said "It would be worth deliberating on the implementation of this."

Neville's team expected an approach overnight, but none came.

I had filed the story to the Irish Daily Star. Next morning, splashed across the front page of the paper, was the bold headline – "Where's my home gone to?" with pictures of Neville and his house. In the courtroom, the press table was packed and I had trouble squeezing in.

Patrick was back in the body of the court, but overnight the vigour had drained from him. His head had dropped. He looked a man who had drawn an unnecessary storm on himself, a storm he would never now be able to calm. The evidence of building contractor John McGinty fuelled that storm.

McGinty was a stocky man with a moustache and an air of determination. He strode into the witness box, clutching a diary from 1993, bristling with a demeanour that indicated a zero tolerance approach to defence barristers.

McGinty described how he had been working for Patrick on the building of Ostán Thoraigh in the months leading up to the destruction of Neville's house. He told the court how knocking down the house was a topic of conversation with Patrick.

McGinty declared: 'Patrick Doohan offered me £1,000 (€1,270) if I'd knock it down. I said I'd consider it. I'd have to have proof he owned the house. The house was directly opposite the hotel. If I owned the hotel, I would like to have it removed.'

Patrick produced no such proof of ownership, so McGinty did not touch the job.

It was with Ó Tuathail's cross-examination of McGinty that the case began its palpable shift away from Patrick. Ó Tuathail suggested there had been a falling-out between Patrick and McGinty as to the pricing of jobs, because of an overpayment made by Patrick. There was a clear hint this was the reason for McGinty's allegations.

McGinty slapped down Ó Tuathail: 'When a house is burnt and your stuff is burnt, it is normal to report it. I'd have expected (the Gardaí) to do something. I'd have supposed there'd have been a forensic team.'

Ó Tuathail suggested that McGinty had been keeping oils in the store that was part of the downstairs of the house. Again McGinty slapped him down, pointing out there was no internal door from the house to the store. Ó Tuathail suggested McGinty was making a claim for damages, a clear hint this was another motivation for his allegations.

Peter Nolan reacted at once and jumped to his feet: 'This is mud-slinging. McGinty is fully entitled to make a claim if he so wishes.' Ó Tuathail conceded this was so.

McGinty got one last dig in at a chastened Ó Tuathail: 'Mr Presho said to me there must be a new Berumuda Triangle on Tory Island – a house just disappears.'

The defence opened its case with evidence from Éamonn Ó Neachtain, who had been manager of the Comharchumann in 1993. Ó Neachtain had flourished after leaving Tory, rising to be Údarás na Gaeltachta Regional Manager for Munster. In an affidavit presented to the court, Neville had named him as one of two men who had allegedly burnt the house.

Ó Neachtain had travelled from Kerry to give evidence. He was a tall man in a grey suit, starting to carry a little weight. He sat in the witness box, removed his metal-framed glasses and looked at judge to tell him that Neville's allegation and other rumours had caused distress to himself and his family. Speaking in Irish, he told the court: 'I came here to deny that false statement. I had no hand or part in what happened.'

Ó Dúlacháin, in his cross-examination of Ó Neachtain, grinned like a cat playing with a mouse. Ó Neachtain remembered the day of the fire. He had heard nothing of it until morning. There was no gossip on the island about it, at the time or afterwards; Justice Murphy interrupted him to tell him this testimony was "strange". At the end of the evidence, Ó Dúlacháin said he wanted to make clear that Ó Neachtain was not accused of being in any way involved in the fire.

Press coverage of the case showed Ó Neachtain had made a tactical blunder in giving evidence. Newspapers, radio and TV reported that a senior Údarás na Gaeltachta official had denied being an arsonist.

(The following day, Ó Neachtain issued a statement to the Kerryman newspaper, saying he had attended the court of his own free will: "I now find myself in the invidious position where my simple denial of any involvement in the case is given such prominence in the media coverage that the general public could be forgiven for thinking that I was centrally involved rather than having a marginal involvement in it. In fact my denial of any involvement became the leading item in much of the media coverage of the case." The tactical wisdom of first coming to court, then issuing such a statement, is questionable).

After Ó Neachtain, the next defence witness was psychiatrist Mick McCaffrey – who probably proved to be Neville's best witness. The previous Saturday, McCaffrey had examined Neville on behalf of Patrick. That interview had lasted for several hours, and McCaffrey was most impressed by Neville's insight into his condition. He said that, whether or not Neville had suffered psychological problems prior to 1993, finding the house had vanished was very injurious to Neville's mental health: 'He was unable to embark on projects and films and complete them successfully – all of these were prior to 1994. After the summer of 1994, I'd be suspicious about his mental health.'

From an unexpected source, this verified Neville's claim that poor health had prevented his instructing a solicitor for many years.

Then the defence called Patrick into the witness box. Patrick had a comprehensive rebuttal to all the allegations of Neville and his legal team, delivered in a fluent and colloquial Irish, littered with English words and phrases, and more than the odd hybrid word (English words made Irish by adding '-áilte' to the end).

More than sixteen years on, his memory of the events of 11th January 1993, two days before the burning, were highly detailed. He remembered the day's stormy weather forcing him to stop working on building the hotel, and the attempts to put the asbestos sheet on the roof of Neville's house — the attempts which ended in the sheet being broken when it accidently hit the wheel of Patrick's digger.

Patrick's wife was pregnant at the time and had developed complications. These meant hospital treatment; a helicopter had to be called to take her to a hospital on the mainland that evening, and Patrick accompanied her. Thus Patrick established he could not have burnt the house as he was not on the island at the time of the fire.

As to McGinty's allegations; not only did Patrick deny them but he had allegations of his own against the contractor. He remembered going to Neville's house where McGinty was in occupation. When he called there he saw a wire hanging from the meter. Over tea on the hotel site, he mentioned this to some of the workmen. They laughed. '"Do you not know that McGinty has the meter bypassed?"' (Patrick used the word "bypassáilte"): 'I'm no electrician but I know

The House that disappeared on Tory Island

there was something that wasn't right.' Thus he was not surprised at the fire, with the implication it was a result of interference with the meter.

Patrick agreed that only those parts of the house made of wood were consumed by the fire. But by that spring it was disappearing quickly. The reason was that no concrete lintels had been used in building it; rather, the lintels were wooden, according to the Tory way of building, and had been burnt away in the fire. This left the walls above the doors and windows unsupported. By the end of that summer, mothers and fathers were worried about its condition, and feared it would fall on the road and injure their children.

Then Patrick turned to the judge with his most important piece of evidence. He had just remembered a date, never recalled before. It was the 19th January 1994. On that day the three gable walls of the house fell in succession, in a domino effect. In the aftermath, Patrick conjured up his fellow-islanders as having been transformed into a Biblical plague of locusts. He graphically described how every morning the people of Tory descended on the site with three tractors and a donkey and cart, loaded up the rubble and took it away for building work.

Patrick moved on to the issue of the septic tank. Neville had never owned the site where the hotel's septic tank was situated. Patrick had bought this site from a Johnny Bán Gallagher. He had put in the septic tank himself, and come across no other tank during the work.

In regard to the car park on the site of Neville's house, this did not exist, as that site was not a car park for the hotel. Patrick had an explanation for the flat area covered with gravel. During construction work on extending the island harbour, the contractor had brought out loads of gravel chips to maintain the island's road. If there were any chips left, the contractor had scattered them on the site of Neville's house, then levelled the site off. He had no idea who had bulldozed the remains of the house onto the foreshore.

As far as the agreement with Neville to provide another site was concerned; he readily admitted signing the document, but said he had never intended to fulfil it because the agreement was not realistic.

Under cross-examination, Patrick strongly denied trespass. Justice Murphy broke in on Ó Dúlacháin's questioning, and set to questioning Patrick himself. In response to the judge's questions, Patrick admitted he had gone onto the site because he had cleared stones from the road onto it. Justice Murphy told him this constituted trespass.

The last minutes of the case finished on high drama. Like the opening, it seemed all would be low-key on the morning of the fourth and final day. The lawyers made their closing submissions. Then Neville asked permission to address the court.

Justice Murphy said 'It is not usual for a plaintiff to give submissions.'

Neville replied 'I'm not normal, your honour.' Patrick's lawyers had no response, except to concede.

This time, Neville was not sworn in as a witness. He told the court that the case was not about retribution, but about restitution.

'We've had the divine hand of God in this court, and we've had the presence of my Heavenly Father and Jesus Christ, his heavenly son,' he said. 'In my sixty-one years of life, I've only heard from my Heavenly Father twice. The first time was in 1980 when I took my girlfriend for a walk in the Dublin mountains. The second time was when I met a Satanist in New Zealand. He attacked me, and I tried to exorcise him. I said: "I bound Satan in the name of Jesus Christ" and he left a free man'

Then he turned to Justice Murphy and asked that they both read from the Book of Isaiah in the King James translation of the Old Testament from the early

17th Century. Lawyers on both sides hesitated, then conferred, visibly unsure how to react. For the first time Ó Tuathail took control of the case; he rose to his feet, said he did not object, and quoted from Bishop Bedell's 17th Century Irish translation of Matthew, Chapter Six, Verse 34 in the New Testament: 'Ba leoir olc an lae sin' ('Sufficient unto the day is the evil thereof'). Justice Murphy agreed to read from the Scripture, but said he would read most verses in silence.

After a couple of minutes reading silently, Justice Murphy began to read the last couple of verses aloud. The last verse read aloud was Verse 21 from Chapter 57: '"There is no peace, sayth my God, to the wicked"'.

Patrick sat slumped a few feet in front of the judge with head bowed – a dejected expression on his face.

Chapter 9

The week following the High Court hearing Neville had the misfortune to make another headline. Gardaí lost him during a 200 kilometre per hour car chase in the early hours of Friday the 13th March. When the Gardaí finally stopped him, he told them: "For half a bottle of wine and two cans of Heineken, that's not bad going."

As a result, Neville was the defendant the next time he appeared in Letterkenny Courthouse. There the District Justice jailed him for two months. The sentence was subsequently reduced on appeal on condition that Neville returned to being a patient in a psychiatric ward of Letterkenny hospital.

Consultant psychiatrist Dr Clifford Haley was one of the doctors treating him during his stay. A former colleague of Neville, then working in RTE, rang the psychiatrist and told him about Neville's filmmaking. The patient Dr Haley was treating seemed to be a completely different man. 'Unless I had been told, I would not have believed that twenty-five years ago he was a major filmmaker,' Dr Haley said.

Neville was still in recovery when, seven weeks after the evidence being heard in Letterkenny, Justice Murphy delivered a ruling on the preliminary issue at the Four Courts in Dublin. This time, there was a big press presence. The Justice delivered the ruling in such a low voice that everybody in court strained to hear. The two most important points went in favour of Neville. Neville's action was in time; the delay beyond the statutory time was caused by illness, which permitted delay:

'On the evidence before me, it appears that, by reason of his mental illness, the Plaintiff was incapable from the date of accrual of the cause of action at least to the date of his instruction to his solicitor which resulted in the letter of 23rd December 2003, of functioning to a degree that would enable him to protect his legal rights in relation to his property as a reasonable man would do.'

Justice Murphy justified this ruling by referring to evidence from both Neville's psychiatrist, Dr Haley, and Patrick's expert witness, Dr McCaffrey:

'(Dr Haley) said a solicitor might refuse to act if the case did not make sense. In July 1994, having realised that his house was gone, his drinking was a pathway to severe illness and highlighted the instability. It was unlikely that one could then do normal business.' Justice Murphy then took the evidence of Dr McCaffrey, and quoted it to justify Neville's claim: 'The return to the island, the finding of the property gone, was very damaging to his mental health. (Dr McCaffrey) would query (Neville's) mental health in 1994. From 1994 to 2000 there was an indication of severe mental illness but (Neville) didn't talk about this.'

Justice Murphy further found Ostán Thoraigh "has and continues to trespass on the plaintiff's property and that the submissions in relation to delay have no bearing on that claim."

Justice Murphy ruled it had not been proved to the satisfaction of the court that Patrick had destroyed the house, but said: 'In the absence of other evidence, the court accepts that Mr Presho's house would have impeded the view from the hotel. The court is satisfied that part of the plantiff's house had been moved to the foreshore, probably mechanically.'

The judgement was critical of the Garda: 'In cross-examination Superintendent McGovern said that none of the original records were available. There was no record of when the gardaí first visited the scene. There was no documentary evidence that anyone was spoken to in 1993.'

So low was Justice Murphy's voice as he read the judgement that some of Neville's legal team misheard, and believed the case lost.

Over the following weeks, the final judgement was expected half a dozen times at the Four Courts. Each time the hearing was opened and adjourned. A second but not final judgement was delivered on the 13th July. Neville was absent, immobilized by depression. Patrick sat slumped forward in the court, an expression of pure misery on his face.

That misery was justified. Justice Murphy opened his judgement saying: 'The Court is satisfied on the analysis of the circumstantial evidence that the plaintiff is entitled to damages for trespass.'

He ruled that Patrick did not have to rebuild the house on the site, but provide either a comparable house on the island, or the open market value of such.

Then he turned to rubbishing Patrick's story about the house being blown down. The judgement was that the house was destroyed in a malicious fire, with no evidence of a collapse:

'The first named defendant's (Patrick) assertion that the property simply collapsed on 19th January 1994, whether by reason of the stormy conditions on or about that date or by reason of unnamed persons removing the stones lacks credibility.'

And Justice Murphy went on to raise questions about Patrick's possible role: 'Photographic evidence of the size of part of the rubble being on the seashore is consistent with the use of a JCB to clear the site. The photographic evidence of the levelled site where the plaintiff's house once stood points to the use of levelling equipment rather than storm collapse and removal by unidentified persons of the remains of the house. Mr Doohan, as the owner of the only JCB on the island had the capacity and opportunity to remove the stones identified by Mr Presho on the foreshore.

The court accepts that the demolition and removal of the house was gradual. The house did not disappear in an instant. The continuance of the process to a gravelled site infers planning and motivation. The court attaches particular importance to the photographic evidence of the uninterrupted view by the hotel of the harbour. ...The court is entitled to infer and is satisfied that it is probable that the first named defendant's JCB, whether driven by the defendant or not, was the only "thing causing the injury".'

Patrick did not just benefit from the demolition because Ostán Thoraigh had gained a clear view of the sea. He also benefited because workers from the mainland stayed free of rent in Neville's house during construction of the hotel.

Patrick was not completely exonerated of McGinty's allegations in regard to his being offered £1,000 (€1.270) by Patrick to demolish the house. The Judge said: 'The court cannot make a finding of fact in relation thereto.'. The 2001 agreement where Neville had proposed to swap his site for one provided by Patrick was evidence in favour of Neville, being judged as " a manifestation of the plaintiff's mental impairment".

The authorities came in for criticism again. Justice Murphy explicitly rejected the evidence of Superintendent McGovern that the Garda investigation was delayed by bad weather stating "The delay in investigation is not adequately explained by adverse weather."

Donegal County Council was the other official body that came under judicial fire. Justice Murphy criticized the "absence of a visit by the local authority until October 1994, and the delay in ascertaining and notifying Mr Presho, then in New Zealand, on 29th April 1994, all contributed to the absence of direct and forensic evidence". He was critical, too, of the islanders for their failure to make statements during the Garda investigation.

A final hearing was fixed for 5th October, when the financial value of the house would be settled. Then, around one o'clock, Patrick's solicitors sent out a fax saying they were appealing to the Supreme Court. This was not acted on at that time.

The final judgement was not delivered until the 10th November 2009. When the case had opened seven months earlier there were only two journalists present; when it finished, the press benches were packed. Some journalists were there as much from personal interest as for work purposes.

Justice Murphy delivered his judgement quickly. He awarded Neville damages of €46,000. The lowest estimate Neville had received from a builder for the reconstruction of his house was €344,731.20.

The judgement was based on the price of a house on Tory. To be fair to the judge, any such price was, by its nature, notional. There were less than a hundred houses on the island. There had been three known sales in the previous ten years . With such a small sample, it was impossible to reliably establish an average price.

The judge refused to order a stay on the payment of damages and costs in the event of an appeal. The damages awarded were a blow to Neville, who was hoping for more. "It wouldn't buy me a chicken coop on Tory Island," was his reaction.

The judgement, however, was a much harder blow to Patrick. Afterwards he sat with his legal team, an unhappy expression on his face, at a table in the restaurant in the courts complex. The eight months had taken a toll on him. His hair was greyer, he no longer looked the Donegal man made good who had strode into the court in Letterkenny the previous March.

Neville's unhappy reaction did not last for long. The judgement gave him a new lease of life. Outside the gates of the court, he spoke to TV and radio. The following day, news of the case went international. In English, it was covered in Britain, the United States, Canada, New Zealand, and the Persian Gulf state of Qatar. Translated into the respective languages, it made headlines in Germany, Iceland, Poland, Sweden, Norway and the Netherlands. Patrick had never before achieved such a level of publicity for Ostán Thoraigh. Whether it was the type of publicity he wanted is doubtful.

Chapter 10

Neville won, despite his poor health, because he refused to give up and accept the injustice done to him. Critical to his success was his legal team who had worked hard on his behalf and was committed to the case.

The Statute of Limitations prevents the taking of legal action more than six years after the act complained of, except where the complainant was under a disability. Neville's team established that he had become ill because of discovering his house had been destroyed. Neville had to wait until a period of relative good health before he could instruct a solicitor.

Without Gillespie, Nolan and Ó Dulacháin mustering the evidence to prove this, the case would have fallen – irrespective of the rights or wrongs of what had been done to Neville. Because the Statute of

Limitations prescribed a shorter period for psychological injuries, Neville was unable to sue for those.

Fifteen years after the house was destroyed, psychiatrist Dr Haley still found Neville "severely unwell... He was very emotionally distressed, and his thinking was disorganized. For someone who had such a high level of day to day functioning, he was really below par." Neville was not able to carry out the tasks of day to day life. He was also unable to give a coherent account of his achievements.

Neville recovered well from that last bout of illness, which had led to his being a patient in Letterkenny hospital. The court victory helped. Before the case, Fiona said: 'I believe he will only have peace of mind and a real improvement in his mental health when he has obtained some form of justice for the deliberate destruction and removal of his home on Tory Island.'

At time of writing, it is uncertain whether Neville has achieved this. He is living with his elderly parents, and is unable to work. The destruction of his house is still casting a shadow over his life. 'It destroyed my life, my marriage, everything,' he says.

There has been widespread sympathy for Neville, which has helped him in his darker times. Despite what he suffered, he has not sought revenge, but restitution. 'It has been a long, hard road but to my knowledge there is no one connected with this affair that I have not forgiven and could (not) now meet, shake their hand and give them a hug,' he said. He took his inspiration from Luke Chapter 6, Verse 37 which states "Judge not and ye shall not be judged: condemn not and ye shall not be condemned: forgive and ye shall be forgiven:"

The public perception of Patrick has been somewhat more negative. The High Court case made him well-known – but not for the right reasons. He is facing a bill of €191,000 for Neville's costs. His own legal bill is unknown, but certainly costly. His dream of a hotel on Tory has faded. Ostán Thoraigh failed to bring the hoped-for economic bonanza to the island. The hotel reported an operating loss of €161,637 for the year to December 31st 2011. Patrick has put the business up for sale or lease – without success to date.

Patrick has also appealed the High Court's judgement to the Supreme Court. This is on the bases that:–

–Neville's complaint should have been struck out as having been made too long after the event;

–the judge expressed bias against the defendant;

The House that disappeared on Tory Island

– the judge made findings contrary to the evidence before him.

He has partially succeeded in an application to have a stay put on the payment of damages. These are not to be paid to Neville. However, Patrick has had to lodge €46,000 into a special account as a condition of proceeding with his appeal. This is to ensure there are sufficient funds to compensate Neville, if the appeal is unsuccessful. The signatories on the account are Neville's solicitor, Gillespie, and Patrick's solicitor, Cannon.

As the Supreme Court operates slowly, the appeal may take several years.

The House that disappeared on Tory Island

The House that disappeared on Tory Island

APPENDIX
Judgments in relation to court case:-
Neville Presho
v
Patrick Doohan and
Ostan Thoraigh and Comhlacht Teoranta

Section One .... The High Court
29th April 2009
Section Two .... The High Court
17th July 2009
Section Three .... The High Court
9th November 2009
Section Four ....The Supreme Court
22nd October 2010

Section One
29th April 2009

THE HIGH COURT

NORTHERN CIRCUIT

COUNTY OF DONEGAL

EQUITY JURISDICTION

BETWEEN/

NEVILLE PRESHO

PLAINTIFF

AND

PATRICK DOOHAN AND OSTAN THORAIGH COMHLACHT TEORANTA

DEFENDANTS

RULING of Mr. Justice Roderick Murphy on preliminary issue delivered 29th April, 2009.

1. Background

Neville Presho, Civil Engineer and documentary film maker, purchased a dwelling house on Tory Island in 1982 and was registered as the owner of Folio 13745F of the Register of Freeholders, County Donegal, on the 27th October, 1982. The property as described in that Folio contained a dwelling house with a septic tank attached. The vendors were Hugh and Mary Doohan who are not related to the first named defendant. Some four years later the plaintiff left Tory Island and resided in New Zealand for eight years until 1994, having boarded up and secured the house which was looked after by a neighbour.

During that time, in or about 1992, the defendants commenced the construction of a hotel premises at the rear of the plaintiff's property which was known as the Tory Island Hotel. The first named defendant employed John McGinty as contractor in late 1992 to November 1993. John McGinty and two of his workers occupied the plaintiff's dwelling house without the consent of the plaintiff while the hotel was being built.

Some time before the 14th January, 1993, during stormy weather an asbestos sheet blew off the house. It is common case that Mr. McGinty and Mr. Doohan with the latter's JCB digger, attempted to replace the asbestos sheet with one provided by the husband of the neighbour who looked after the house. This was not possible as the replacement sheet was broken as it fell on or was broken by the wheel of the JCB digger. There is conflict of evidence as to how the replacement sheet was broken. It is not controverted that at that stage the workman left Mr. Presho's house and stayed at the local hostel. Mr. McGinty said that he had removed the electricity supply fuses.

In the early hours of the morning of the 14th January, 1993, a fire substantially damaged Mr. Presho's house. Mr. Doohan was not on the island. The matter was reported to the gardai by Mr. McGinty on 15th who said that his equipment and fuel had been destroyed.

Subsequently further damage was caused to the house. Mr. McGinty said that there was only one digger on the island. He said that he didn't see Mr. Doohan or anyone else remove stones.

Superintendent McGovern gave evidence of the complaint of Mr. McGinty, who was satisfied that the fire was malicious, which was recorded in a Crime Report Document. The first contact by Mr. Presho was on 27th July 1994 at Bunbeg garda station who could not point to a suspect.

Mr. Presho produced photographs which had been obtained from Donegal County Council. On 21st November 1994 Mr. Presho wrote to Sergeant Friel asking that the investigation not be pursued, that he forgave those who burnt his house. Sergeant Friel's report noted a "peculiar conversation" that Mr. Presho had a premonition that the roof would be blown off. It was an act of God.

However on 13th August 2003 Mr. Presho sent correspondence to the Garda Commissioner in relation to the investigation referring to difficulties with Mr. Doohan. The matter was referred to Detective Garda Moore in Glenties who met with Mr. Presho at Tarryfinn airport on 19th September 2003 where a first statement of complaint was made. Detective Garda Moore investigated the matter and interviewed all persons mentioned. Mr. McGinty declined to make a statement but swore an affidavit which corresponded to the evidence he gave to the court. Mr. Doohan wrote a memo. All 14 others declined to make a statement. There was no evidence to warrant any charge.

Mr. Presho then made a complaint to the Garda Complaints Board. On 12th May 2006 this complaint was deemed inadmissible on the basis of delay.

An internal review was undertaken by Superintendent McGowan and Sergeant Carroll who re-interviewed Mr. Doohan and others. A report was made on 7th November 2007 which concluded that there was no basis for a criminal investigation. By then all the gardaí involved had retired.

In cross-examination Superintendent McGovern said that none of the original records were available. There was no record of when the gardaí first visited the scent. There was no documentary evidence that anyone as spoken to in 1993. In July 1994 Mr. Presho had reported the disappearance of his house which was a different incident to the fire. A video and photographs were given to the gardaí. The latter showed building debris including large stones on the foreshore which was identified by Mr. Presho as part of the porch of his former house. There was no evidence to the contrary. The court is satisfied that part of the plaintiff's house had been moved to the foreshore probably mechanically.

An appointment was made with Sergeant Friel to go to Tory Island prior to 21st November 1994 but according to Sergeant Friel's report was cancelled by Mr. Presho. There was no evidence that Mr. Doohan was involved in the removal of the house. It was noted on the garda file that, subsequently, he had a contract with Donegal County Council to remove the rubble from the road between Mr. Presho's house and the hotel.

There were theories as to what had happened but the gardai could not react to suspicion.

In the absence of forensic investigation there was no evidence that the fire was malicious.

Mr. Charlie Cannon, executive engineer of Donegal County Council, had faxed a manuscript letter dated 19th January, 1994 to the first name defendant regarding the blocked County Road on Tory Island as follows:

"Dear Pat,

As per our telephone conversation of earlier today, I would be obliged if you could clear the blocked County Road on Tory Island as soon as possible using the excavator which you have available on site, all I want done is the road made passable, which would mean pushing the stones debris, (s/c) into the side where the existing derelict building is. You can forward your bill to the above address for payment.

Charlie Cannon."

On the 29th April, 1994, some fifteen months after the fire, Mr. Presho received a letter from Donegal County Council as follows:-

> "Re: Dangerous Building at Tory Island
>
> Dear Mr. Presho,
>
> It has been brought to out attention that a building owned by you on Tory Island is in a dangerous condition.
>
> There is a new hotel being built adjacent to this building and the owners are concerned that same will be a danger to the public as well as being unsightly (see attached photograph).
>
> Under the Derelict Sites Act 1990, Donegal County Council are required to take whatever action is necessary to render this building safe. Storm damage has also taken its toll on this building and considerable damage has been caused.
>
> I would be grateful if you could let us know what your intentions are regarding this property, before we proceed to enter the same on the Register of Derelict Sites.
>
> Yours sincerely,
>
> For County Secretary"

Mr. Presho said that he returned to Ireland on the 5th July, 1994, and, before going to Tory Island, wrote to Donegal County Council. A few days later he and his wife, whom he had married in April 1990, took the ferry to Tory Island. As they entered the harbour at Middletown where the house had been situated he could not see his house. It was not there. He did see the hotel which was to the rear of where his house once stood. He could not believe it. He had planned to stay in the house and stayed with their next door neighbour with whom they had previously stayed before they bought the house. He produced a photograph which he had taken from the front of the hotel which showed an uninterrupted view of the harbour. He superimposed a scaled card representing the outline of his house upon that photograph. This blocked the entire view from the hotel. In the absence of other evidence the court accepts that Mr. Presho's house would have impeded the view from the hotel.

A number of whitewashed boulders had been placed around where the house had once stood. The site including the site of the septic tank had been levelled.

He asked Mr. Doohan, the first named defendant, what had happened and was told to find out who had set fire to the house.

One of the islanders told him that it was better that he did not ask.

His neighbour to whom he had asked to look after the house and with whom he was then staying said she saw nothing and that the house had been sucked up in a whirlwind.

He had found out that the defendant's contractor, Mr. McGinty had reported the fire to the gardai and that he had lost plant and equipment valued at £3,000 in the fire.

Mr. Presho's evidence was that Mr. McGinty had informed him that, at the early stages of the development of the hotel, Mr. Doohan had offered Mr. McGinty £1,000 to demolish Mr. Presho's house. Mr. McGinty's evidence to the court was to that effect but that he refused to do so until he was certain who owned the house. He said he was asked to price a new septic tank for the hotel but that Mr. Doohan used his JCB to do that work himself.

Mr. Presho said that the site of his house was being used as a car park and as the site for a septic tank for the hotel. Mr. Doohan denied such use.

The court is satisfied from the photographs of Mr. Presho that the site was available to the hotel for that purpose. The investigation and plans produced by the plaintiff's architects as to the route of the inflow to the septic tank, which appear to deviate from the grant of planning, are not controverted and substantiate trespass.

He went to Donegal County Council offices in Lifford and met Cecelia McGovern who had written the letter on behalf of the County Secretary. She produced letters from people complaining of stones from his house on the road between his house and the hotel and the letter of the Council to Mr. Doohan dated 19th January, 1994, referred to above.

Mr. Presho in his evidence described how the incident had caused him distress. He said that "a switch had flicked in his mind" and there was a knot in his stomach when he realised that his house had gone. He began to drink heavily.

He then went to Dublin with his wife to the Land Registry. The Folio was missing. He contacted the solicitor who had acted for him and whom he had known for ten years. He said that solicitor refused to take on his case. He had spent two months in Ireland away from his family. He said he felt he was coming up against closed doors and his mind had changed. His wife became extremely fearful of him.

On the 20th September, 1994, he went to his General Practitioner who referred him to a psychiatrist who diagnosed bi-polar mood disorder as the cause of his breakdown. He was committed to care in a psychiatric hospital and on medication for several months.

In 1995, his wife became ill and his remaining children were taken into care. He said he was barely able to cope with life. He became depressed and suicidal. He told the court he did not have the courage to do it and by 2000, felt he was like zombie having received electric treatment and being locked up in psychiatric units.

He described the strong emotional effect of Tory Island on him. He was unemployable and not in a fit state mentally.

He stayed with his family in Northern Ireland and spent several periods in psychiatric care having been sectioned (certified). He was on medication. He was depressed and suicidal.

His wife felt that he needed closure but he did not have the heart to proceed as it was opening up old wounds.

Subsequently, in April 2000 he returned to Tory. He asked if any one knew what happened to his house. He gave evidence to the court that nobody would say anything. The site was covered with chippings and was then being used as a car park for the hotel. The septic tank of the hotel was where his septic tank was. He referred to photographs which he had taken subsequently.

There followed a curious agreement dated 4th October 2001 preceded by two short letters. The plaintiff had written to the first named defendant on 17th August, 2001, in the following terms:

> "A Chara,
>
> Can you please remove the two white stones immediately in front of Ostán Thoraigh, as they are resting on my house site, without my permission.
>
> Thanking you, in advance.
>
> Mise le meas,
>
> Neville Presho"

The following day the first named defendant replied as follows:

> "Dear Neville,

Further to our conversation in the clubhouse last night I regret that I didn't come across the copy fax from Donegal County Council, but I can confirm that I cleared the road from rock, stones, and debris to make the road passable as instructed by Donegal County Council.

Yours sincerely,

Pat Doohan, 18/8/01."

The plaintiff's notice of his application to the planning authority was published in the "Derry People" in "Donegal News" on Friday, September 21st, 2001. It read:

"I, Neville Presho, am applying for planning permission for the erection of a two-storey replacement dwelling at Middletown, Tory Island.

The agreement of 4th October, 2001, read as follows:

"We, the undersigned Neville Presho and P. Doohan do hereby this day 2001

enter into a binding agreement, where I P. Doohan will secure the land rights

to the area shown shaded, for Neville Presho and will assign to him the land, rights and ownership

of that area. In pursuance, I Neville Presho will simultaneously assign the land rights and ownership

of the land known as folio 13745F in O.S. 6 Donegal to Patrick Joseph Doohan of Ostan Thoraigh.

This is a straight swap transaction and does not involve any fanancial (sic) remuneration to either party.

Agreed at Tory on 4/10/2001, signed Neville Presho

signed P. Doohan.

witnessed Angela Duggan, runai, Cumharchumann Thorai.

This was accompanied by a sketch signed by the three, the two parties and witnessed by Angela Duggan which showed a hatched round undetermined area beside the Community Centre.

Also included was a draft undated statement with the plaintiffs address in Hollywood, Co. Down and telephone numbers which stated as follows:

"It gives me great pleasure, as proprietor of Óstán Thoraigh to fully endorse Neville Presho's plans for a Tory visitor centre (illegible). His ideas and enthusiasm will ensure that Tory becomes a major tourist attraction in Ireland.

The ferry, the smooth operator TM will be 150 seat, state-of-the-art high speed wave (illegible) catamarand, designed to the specifications of skipper Jimmy Sweeney to suit the sea conditions around Tory. It will out trawl (?) time between Magherety to Tory from the current one hour to little under 20 minutes. In addition the ride in all sea conditions will be extremely stable.

I was involved in Mr. Presho's film Oilean about life in Tory Island in 1976 and have enjoyed discussing ideas with him up to the present."

A further letter to the first name defendant from the plaintiff dated 20th June, 2003, from Hollywood, Co. Down read as follows:

"Dear Patrick,

This letter has been sent by registered mail.

When I met you on Tory Island in October, 2001, we both signed a legally binding document in which you were to acquire a site (marked) on the island, in exchange for you acquiring my house site.

As I had not heard from you since we signed that document on 4/10/01, I then wrote to you on 6/3/02 and again, received no response from you.

You are hereby advised to expedite this matter within the next 21 days.

Failure to do so, will result in this issue being taken out of my hands.

Best wishes,

Yours sincerely,

Neville Presho.

A final letter dated 4th August, 2003, enclosed €100 which Mr. Doohan had lent Mr. Presho and referred to and enclosed a letter in relation to an unrelated matter.

He was referred to a solicitor and began investigating the cause of the removal of his house. A letter intimating legal action was sent to the defendants on 23rd December 2003. A plenary summons issued on 3rd January 2006 over two years later seeking, *inter alia*, an order setting aside the purported agreement of 4th October, 2001.

2. Pleadings

In that plenary summons, dated the 3rd January, 2006, the plaintiff claimed damages for trespassing and interference with his property together with unlawful and continued unauthorised use of his property; an order that the defendants restore the dwelling house and remove their septic tank. In addition the plaintiff sought an order setting aside and declaring null and void a purported agreement made between the plaintiff and the first named defendant concerning the plaintiff's property dated the 4th October, 2001.

In the statement of claim, delivered one year later on 13th February, 2007, the plaintiff pleaded that he had applied for outline planning permission to rebuild his house in September, 2001, and alleged that, shortly thereafter, on the 4th October, 2001, the defendant approached him and attempted to enter an agreement on that day purporting to be an exchange of land rights with no financial remuneration which was signed by the plaintiff whose signature was witnessed by the secretary of the Tory Island Co-Operative. The plaintiff alleges that at no time had he independent legal advice in relation to his agreement.

The plaintiff alleges that his house had been pushed over the bank "and on to the foreshore" and that boulders had been placed to form a boundary around the land for the purpose of securing a car park which was used for the benefit of the defendants' hotel without the consent and permission of the plaintiff. The plaintiff pleaded that the defendant was aware that the plaintiff's house blocked the sea view of the hotel. It was alleged that the defendant's servants and their agents had wrongfully, illegally and unlawfully removed the dwelling house of the plaintiff and taken possession of plaintiff's lands and property and were wrongfully claiming the said lands.

The plaintiff's reply to particulars stated that the manic depression of the plaintiff was first diagnosed in mid-September 1994 by a Dr. Tom O'Flynn. The plaintiff was never made a ward of court. Evidence of his psychiatric and medical condition and treatment would be provided at the hearing of the case. The document of the 4th October, 2001, was signed on that date by the plaintiff and the first named defendant at a time when the plaintiff was undergoing treatment.

3. Defence

By defence dated the 2nd January, 2007, the defendants pleaded that the plaintiff was not entitled to the relief claimed or any relief because of lengthy and inexcusable delay.

The defendants relied on the provisions of the Statute of Limitations as a bar to the plaintiff's claim. If the plaintiff did suffer the alleged or any damage or incurred loss so as to bar the plaintiff's claim against any other person then, it was pleaded, the plaintiff should be held to be responsible for the acts of such a person within the meaning of s. 35(1)(i) of the Civil Liability Act 1961 (as amended).

In passing the court observes that s. 35 relied on in the defence provides for the determination of contributory negligence by a plaintiff and extends to a person from whom the plaintiff is vicariously liable to include a personal representative being responsible for the contributory negligence of the act of the deceased or of a beneficiary. The provision relied on is as follows:

"(i) where the plaintiff's damage was caused by concurrent wrongdoers and the plaintiff's claim against one wrongdoer has been barred by the Statute of Limitations or any other limitation enactment, the plaintiff should be deemed to be responsible for the acts of such wrongdoer."

As there is no defence of contributory negligence nor, indeed, any evidence of contributory negligence, it would appear that this defence is not relevant.

In any event no argument nor submission was made in relation thereto.

The defence admits that the first named defendant is the beneficial owner of the hotel premises the title to which is registered in the name of the second named defendant which is a company controlled by the first named defendant.

However, the defendants denied that the contractor employed by the first named defendant, John McGinty, was approached by the first named defendant and requested to knock down the house of the plaintiff for payment and to dig out the septic tank on the plaintiff's lands replacing it with a septic tank for the new hotel premises as alleged.

It was further denied that the first named defendant had placed his workmen living in the premises of the plaintiff without consent or authority of the plaintiff or that he or his servants or agents had removed roof sheets of the seaward side of the plaintiff's house and stopped intended repairs to the said house by Mr. McGinty the contractor, thereby allowing ingress of water to the plaintiff's house and making it inhabitable.

The defendants denied taking wrongfully or unlawfully possession of the lands or placing a septic tank on the lands for the purpose of the use of the hotel. The defendants further denied that they had unlawfully trespassed upon the plaintiff's property.

The defendants denied that the plaintiff's property was slowly and by degrees demolished by the first named defendant. Mr. Doohan did not approach Donegal County Council in an attempt to have the building fully demolished. He did not demolish the dwelling house or clear the site. The defendant admits however, that he cleared the stones or debris from the road at the request of Donegal County Council.

The defendants admitted that there was some discussion at one stage between the parties in relation to the document dated 4th October, 2001, but denied that these discussions took place at the behest of the first named defendant.

4. Statute of Limitations on delay

Counsel on behalf of the defendants had raised a preliminary issue regarding the Statute of Limitations.

The allegation made by the plaintiff was that the first named defendant arranged unnamed persons to set the defendant's house alight on 14th January, 1993. The first intimation of a proposed legal action was received on 23rd December, 2003. A plenary summons issued on 3rd January, 2006.

The defendants submitted that an action founded on tort could not be brought after the expiration of six years from the date on which the cause of action accrued.

The exception to the six year rule provided for by s. 49 of the Statute of Limitations 1957, relates to a person being under a disability including being of unsound mind. A person shall be conclusively presumed to be of unsound mind where he is detained in pursuance of any enactment authorising the detention of persons of unsound mind or criminal lunatics. (Section 48 (2)).

Section 49 (1)(a) provides as follows:

> "If, on the date when any right of action accrued for which a period of limitation is fixed by this Act, the person to whom it accrued was under a disability, the action may, subject to the subsequent provisions of the section, be brought at any time before the expiration of six years from the date when the person ceased to be under a disability or died, whichever event first occurred notwithstanding that the period of limitations has expired."

There is no definition of unsound mind in the Act.

Rowan v. Bord na Mona [1990] 2 I.R. 425 followed *Kirby v. Leather* [1965] 2 Q.B. 367. In both cases the plaintiff suffered injuries because of an accident which gave rise to his cause of action. A plaintiff who was injured on the day by the tort can rely on section 49. In the present case, the defendant submitted that the reply to particulars stated that manic depression was first diagnosed in mid-September, 1994, which was the year following the fire and following the plaintiff's return to Tory Island on or about 5th July, 1994.

The plaintiff further submits that though the concept of unsound mind is undefined in statute, *Kirby v. Leather* referred to a proper and reasonable meaning for the phrase related to a person who by reason of mental disorder was incapable of managing and administering his property and affairs. The plaintiff further relied on *McDonald v. McBain* [1991] 1 I.R. 284.

It was submitted by the defendants that the plaintiff was suffering an illness of a temporary character. The onus rested on the plaintiff to prove that he was of unsound mind as these were matters which were peculiarly within the knowledge of the plaintiff. (*McGowan v. Carvill* [1960] 1 I.R. 330 at 336).

In relation to delay the defendant referred to *Primor* (1992 I.R. 459) and concluded that there had been inordinate and inexcusable delay.

5. Consideration of preliminary issue

5.1 On the question of unsound mind, Lord Denning M.R. in *Kirby v. Leather* [1965] 2 Q.B. 367 held:

> "It seems to me that the words 'unsound mind' in a statute must be construed in relation to the subject matter with which the statute is dealing. In *Whysall v. Whysall* [1959] 3 WLR 592, Phillimore J. held that the phrase 'unsound mind' in a statute relating to the dissolution of marriage must be taken to describe a mental state which would justify a dissolution of the marriage tie, that is, mental incapacity such as to

make it impossible for a couple to live a normal married life together. So here it seems to me in this statute a person is of 'unsound mind' when he is, by reason of mental illness, incapable of managing his affairs in relation to the accident as a reasonable man would do. It is similar to the test where a guardian ad litem or next friend is appointed under the new R.S.C. Ord. 80. r.1. That states that a person under a disability means 'a person who by reason of mental disorder is incapable of managing and administering his property and affairs.' So here it seems to me that David Kirby was of unsound mind if he was, by reason of mental illness, incapable of managing his affairs in relation to this accident."

In determining if mental disorder or illness amounts to a disability for the purpose of the Statute of Limitations, the test is whether or not the plaintiff was capable of managing his affairs in relation to the alleged wrong. Managing his affairs includes the protection of his legal rights.

5.2 Counsel for the defendant argues that the date of the accrual of the cause of action was the 14th January 1993, the date on which the plaintiff alleges that the first named defendant arranged for unnamed persons to set the defendant's house alight.

Counsel for the plaintiff submits that the cause of action for damage to the plaintiff's property accrued at its earliest in July 1994 when the combination of evidence gave rise to a legitimate concern that the defendants were responsible for the damage. The Plaintiff bases this argument on the fact that he did not know of the malicious nature of the fire or the destruction of his property.

The plaintiff was told by the defendant, Mr. Doohan that "he should find out who burnt his property". He found out, on visiting the Garda station in Bunbeg on the

20th July 1994, that a report of malicious damage had been made. He met Mr. McGinty the subcontractor and heard what he had to say. He visited Donegal County Council offices and established that they were not involved in demolishing his house.

In this regard, the Plaintiff relies on Section 71(1)(b) of the Statute of Limitations which states that in certain cases of concealment time does not begin to run. He submits that the real issue is not when the fire occurred or when the property was demolished and levelled but on what date it could be said that the Plaintiff knew that the fire or levelling was malicious. The Plaintiff relies on the judgment of Morris J. in *McDonald v. McBain* [1991] 1 IR 284, a case involving a malicious house fire, where he held:

> "It is my opinion that if the circumstances were such that the plaintiff in the present case had her property destroyed by fire deliberately by a third party and that third party, either by stealth or silence, succeeded in hiding that fact from the plaintiff, and she was left in complete and total ignorance of the identity of the wrongdoer, then that conduct on the part of the wrongdoer would amount to fraud within the meaning of the Statute of Limitations."

I am satisfied on the facts before me that the Plaintiff is correct in submitting that the cause of action did not accrue before he returned to Tory Island in July 1994. Indeed the cause of action could not accrue until he discovered the identity of the wrongdoer.

There was evidence of concealment by way of silence by those interviewed in the garda investigation. There was further evidence of concealment, to some extent, in April 2000 when the plaintiff returned to the island and got no answers from the unidentified islanders with whom he spoke.

This postponed the accrual of the action against the defendants in general or against the first named defendant in particular as malicious intent can only be imputed against a corporate body through its director(s).

McDonald v. McBain applies to the extent that the plaintiff was left in complete and total ignorance of the identity of a wrongdoer. The evidence that the plaintiff "got the whole story" in July 1994 from Mr. McGinty was to the effect that Mr. McGinty had been approached by the first named defendant to demolish the house but not as to who maliciously destroyed it. This was denied by that defendant.

Moreover, the attitude of the plaintiff regarding the purported agreement of 4th October 2001 between the defendant and himself does not indicate that that defendant was identified as a wrongdoer at that time.

While it may be that the plaintiff was not in "complete and total ignorance of the identify of a wrongdoer" in the words of *McDonald v. McBain* there is no doubt that there is an overlapping issue as to whether the plaintiff was under a disability at the time the cause of action occurred.

5.3   It follows that it is necessary to determine the extent to which the plaintiff was under a disability by reason of being of unsound mind on the date of accrual of the cause of action whatever that date might have been. In this regard the evidence of the two psychiatrists is relevant.

Dr. Clifford Halley, clinical director of Donegal-Letterkenny Hospital where the plaintiff had been under his care from mid-January 2009, gave evidence of his contact with Dr. Watson, a consultant from Northern Ireland who had treated the plaintiff. He concurred in her diagnosis that the plaintiff had been in a manic state consistent with bi-polar disorder, that he was depressed, disruptive and suicidal and his judgment was impaired.

He said that while the first documented diagnosis of this illness was in 1994, he was of the view that it was quite unusual to have the onset in mid-forties as Mr. Presho then was rather than in early to mid-twenties to thirties.

Dr. Halley said the plaintiff had suffered from a very severe episode and was seriously ill. The signs were hard to detect. They were more irrational and hard to present matters in a logical and coherent manner. It was a relapsing illness very vulnerable to different life situations. There was also evidence of a failure to adhere to treatment.

In its manic phase a patient feels super-human with urgent action required and exceeds socially unacceptable behaviour. In the depressive phase the smallest problems can be insurmountable.

It was not possible to manage that illness in an open ward. Medication to control mood swings was necessary. The plaintiff had to be detained against his will.

There was no single factor triggering bi-polar disorder but psycho-social triggers affected one's behaviour.

The phrase "a person of unsound mind" was not often used outside courts and was not therefore helpful.

Medication requires close monitoring and he was required, when in Northern Ireland, to be hospitalised. Dr. Halley said he saw him in an episode of mania. His thoughts were grandiose, that he had a special mission in life and religious beliefs became overwhelming. The evidence relating to the interpretive centre was symptomatic and would make one worry about the mental health of the plaintiff.

In cross-examination he said that he took the history from Dr. Watson but had not contact with the psychiatrist in New Zealand. Dr. Watson had dealt with the plaintiff over the last five years.

Dr. Halley said he couldn't get the plaintiff's consent at first to access the records from Dr. Watson.

He said the depressive phase could be more prolonged and required months' hospitalisation; in the worst case scenario it could be six months every year in a depressive phase while the patient would be able to get along in a normal way, unless there were permanent damage which had not been prepared. Dr. Halley said it was difficult to pronounce on in his mental state in 1993.

He said that a solicitor might refuse to act if the case did not make sense. In July 1994 having realised that his house was gone his drinking was a pathway to severe illness and highlighted the instability. It was unlikely that one could then do normal business.

Dr. Brian McCaffrey, consultant psychiatrist, gave evidence on behalf of the defendants.

Dr. McCaffrey said he didn't have access to records other than that he knew that the plaintiff had bi-polar disorder in 1994. When he interviewed him he queried the late onset of the illness. The plaintiff was helpful and intelligent and described his childhood illnesses. His father, a Presbyterian Minister, had gone from Glasgow to Hollywood, Co. Down when the plaintiff was ten. At age fourteen he had a head injury, was depressed for four months but recovered. He studied civil engineering but, Dr. McCaffrey believed, would have been better conceptually in architecture.

He described his films. In 1974 the "Summer Silver" documentary in Bunbeg was a success but his mood took a nose dive. He had been severely depressed in 1984 – a ten year cycle.

In 1994 he was in a mental health facility in South Island, New Zealand and recovered. By 1999 things deteriorated when he was in Northern Ireland where he as sectioned (committed) and was put on medication with which he was not compliant. Continuous treatment was necessary to decrease the severity and frequency of his illness.

The plaintiff's evidence regarding the description of his illness was clear. The only difference he had with Dr. Halley's evidence was that he believed the onset to be earlier than 1994. Dr. Halley had commented that late-onset was unusual and that's why Dr. McCaffrey went back further. He was satisfied that the plaintiff was not malingering. He had lost three out of thirteen years through depression. He believed that recovery could be complete between illnesses. He felt frustrated. His mood swings veered from desperation to forgiveness.

In cross-examination he agreed that no single event caused bi-polar disorder. It need not last a life time and can sometimes burn out. It required ongoing management and assessment, sometimes as frequently as weekly or bi-monthly.

He agreed that Mr. Presho had an intensity of attachment in relation to his relationship with islands generally and Tory in particular. The return to the island and the finding of the property gone was very damaging to his mental health. He would query his mental health in 1994. From 1994 to 2000 there was an indication of severe medical illness but he didn't talk of this. His children had been taken into care and his wife was ill. He deteriorated in 1999. He was sectioned (certified) in Northern Ireland and was afraid that he would be kept locked up for the rest of his life.

Dr. McCaffrey described his two hour interview as a snapshot which he believed would require two to three days. He remarked that Mr. Presho said that it would require two to three weeks.

Dr. McCaffrey believed that the written agreement of 4th October, 2001, with Mr. Doohan after a night of exposure on the hill on Tory Island was a sign of mental illness.

6. Decision on preliminary issue

Evidence was heard by the court by the Plaintiff that he was diagnosed as suffering from bi-polar disorder in September 1994, when he had returned to New Zealand. He was then in his 40s. Dr. Halley thought it was unusual to have such a late onset of such illness. Dr. McCaffrey, having met Mr. Presho for some two hours and who had probed his early history was of the opinion that the condition pre-dated the diagnosis. Both psychiatrists described the key features of mania being a frantic outburst of activity combined with a failure to have the energy to see tasks through. The Plaintiff himself gave evidence of having been shocked by the incidents of July 1994, describing this as a "switch having flicked in his mind" and leading him to drink heavily. He had spent two months in Ireland away from his family and when he returned to New Zealand his wife was fearful of him. He sought medical help in September 1994. Between 1994 and 2000, the Plaintiff suffered from mental instability, repeated hospitalisation, detention, and ongoing medication and alcohol dependency. His children were taken into care and only returned on condition that the

Plaintiff agreed to be deported from New Zealand. Throughout this period, the Plaintiff was incapable of meaningful employment.

Dr. Halley was of the view that it was possible that he may not have made any sense when he consulted a solicitor.

I am satisfied from the medical evidence that it is probable that the plaintiff had suffered the onset of bi-polar disorder before the discovery of the disappearance of his house on Tory Island.

If I am incorrect in this finding it is clear that from his own evidence and the surrounding circumstance of his visit to the island in July 2004 that this disorder manifested itself at the time of that discovery as the flicking of a switch. *Kirby v. Leather* and *Rowan v. Bord Na Mona* applied.

His reactions and behaviour in relation to the causation of the fire, demolition of the house, trespass on the site and seeking redress varied from frustration to forgiveness. The letter to the gardai on 21st November 1994 to halt the investigation and the cancelling of the prior appointment with Sergeant Friel, in addition appeared to be wholly irrational.

Nonetheless he did instruct his solicitor to write a letter to the defendants and to issue a summons two years later on 3rd January, 2006. The court expresses a concern regarding his reply to particulars he stated that he was not diagnosed until September 1994 as suffering from bi-polar disorder. Notwithstanding the court accepts that it was probable that the onset was earlier.

On the evidence before me, it appears that, by reason of his mental illness, the Plaintiff was incapable from the date of accrual of the cause of action at least to the date of his instructions to his solicitor which resulted in the letter of 23rd December 2003, of functioning to a degree that would enable him to protect his legal rights in relation to his property as a reasonable man would do. In this regard, I am guided by the finding of the Court of Appeal in *Kirby v. Leather* [1965] 2 QB 367, where the plaintiff therein had also approached a solicitor within the limitation period but had not, by reason of mental illness, taken the step of commencing an action in relation to the incident. It is clear in the current case that the Plaintiff's illness, characterised by periods of mania alternated with periods of depression, meant that he was not in a fit state to look after his affairs and to vindicate his legal rights.

In the event of the findings of concealment and if disability the court concludes, on the preliminary issue that the defendants are not entitled to an order dismissing the plaintiff's claim on the grounds of delay.

Having heard the evidence and considered the submissions on the merits of the case the court is satisfied that the second named defendant has and continues to trespass on the plaintiff's property and that the submissions in relation to delay have no bearing on that claim.

The court invited the parties to consider an amendment to the pleadings, on such terms as the court may deem proper, to consider whether, and to what extent, any remedy for unjust enrichment may be appropriate.

Section Two

17th July 2009

THE HIGH COURT

2006 4 P

BETWEEN/

NEVILLE PRESHO

PLAINTIFF

AND
PATRICK DOOHAN AND ÓSTAN THORAIGH
COMHLACHT TEORANTA

DEFENDANTS

JUDGMENT of Mr. Justice Roderick Murphy on substantive issue delivered the 17th July, 2009.

1. Preliminary issue determined

On 3rd April, 2009, the court ruled in favour of the plaintiff on a preliminary issue. The pleadings and complex facts of the case are referred to in that decision. The issue was whether, in the circumstance of the plaintiff's bi-polar disorder, the defendants could rely on the Statute of Limitations and delay. Further hearings were held in relation to damages and unjust enrichment including the final hearing on 13th July, 2009.

2. Substantive claim

The plaintiff's house was damaged by fire in unexplained circumstances prior to 8.00 am on the morning of 14th January, 1993. The court also accepts that the physical structure was significantly altered between 14th January, 1993 and the visit of a County Council Engineer on 7th October, 1993, nine months later. It would appear that the remaining structure was removed off the site by the date of the opening of the second named defendant's hotel on 11th May, 1994 at which time the plaintiff's site was levelled and the septic tank destroyed or covered over. Certainly when Mr. and Mrs. Presho returned two months after the hotel had opened, on 5th July 1994, there was no trace of the house.

Mr. Presho had been sent a photo from the County Council of the damaged house on 29th April, 1994. It was unclear when the photo was taken.

It was alleged that an offer had been made by Mr. O'Neachtain, the manager of the co-operative for the purchase of the plaintiff's property in 1992 before the hotel site was brought on 10th June, 1993 for £1,000. The plaintiff submits that the only logical basis for that was that the manager was acting for the defendants. This was denied by the manager. No other evidence was adduced. In the circumstance the court is not in a position to determine whether an offer had or had not been made.

The court accepts the evidence that the property was a 19th Century stone building of a strong and durable nature and that it had before 14th January, 1993 lost part of its roof. The first named defendant's assertion that the property simply collapsed on 19th January, 1994 whether by reason of the stormy conditions on or about that date or by reason of unnamed persons removing the stones lacks credibility. The evidence that he was the only person on the island with a JCB was not controverted. There was no evidence adduced to support the assertion that the building collapsed.

Photographic evidence of the size of part of the rubble being on the seashore is consistent with the use of a JCB to clear the site. The photographic evidence of the levelled site where the plaintiff's house once stood points to the use of levelling equipment rather than storm collapse and removal by unidentified persons of the remains of the house.

The septic tank serving the hotel appears to run across the path of the plaintiff's septic tank. The court accepts the evidence of the plaintiff and of Mr. Hyde, Architect, in this regard.

Mr. John McGinty, who had acted as a building contractor or subcontractor employed by the defendants in relation to the building of the hotel. He asserted that he had been asked by Mr. Doohan to demolish the plaintiff's house and offered £1,000 to do so. This was contradicted by Mr. Doohan in his evidence. Mr. McGinty refused to demolish the house, without, as he said, having written proof of ownership. The court cannot make a finding of fact in relation thereto.

The statement of claim pleaded that Mr. Doohan, the first named defendant and the principal of the second named company, placed his workmen in the plaintiff's house from 1992 to 1993. Mr. McGinty, who was a building contractor employed by the defendants to build Óstan Thoraigh, the hotel, says that he stayed in the plaintiff's house with the approval of the caretaker, Mary Meenan. Ms. Meenan did not give evidence. I accept the evidence of Mr. Presho that she had no authority to allow the defendants' contractors to occupy the premises. The court accepts that the defendants' contractor and the defendants benefited.

It was alleged that Mr. Doohan took sheeting off the roof and hindered repairs. One of Mr. McGinty's workmen gave specific evidence that the sheet came off in what he described as "a hurricane". The court accepts that there was no evidence that Mr. Doohan removed the sheeting. It was pleaded that Mr. Doohan stopped/hindered repairs. The court is not satisfied that this was so. The evidence given was that he assisted with repairs but that the replacement sheet was broken while being replaced by Mr. Doohan's JCB in weather conditions described as blowing "around like a parachute". The court accepts that Mr. Doohan helped weigh the roof down with sandbags and ropes in difficult conditions and did not hinder the attempted repair.

It was alleged that the fire was malicious and was allegedly caused by an electrical fault. Mr. McGinty had stored some combustibles in the house. Mr. McGinty believed but gave no reason for his belief that the fire was malicious other than that the fuses had been removed before the fire. The court, on the balance of probability, accepts that the fire was malicious and was exacerbated by the presence of combustibles.

No evidence was offered for the allegation that two persons acting as agents for the defendants had set the fire. The allegation was withdrawn against Mr. O'Neachtain in open court. Nobody gave evidence that the fire was started by the defendant or his agents. Mr. Doohan gave evidence to the contrary and said that he was not on the island at the time. I accept the evidence of the defendants.

It was suggested in the statement of claim that the gardaí did not investigate the fire and destruction of the house. The evidence given by Superintendent Eugene McGovern was that once Mr. McGinty complained on 15th January, 1993, the Garda investigation was delayed by bad weather and was then inconclusive. When Mr. Presho complained over a year later in July 1994 a further investigation took place. No evidence was forthcoming to the Gardaí which would warrant a prosecution. The absence of statements from the many inhabitants regarding what should have been obvious to all, is significant. The delay in investigation is not adequately explained by adverse weather.

It was alleged that the building was subsequently demolished by degrees by the defendants. No evidence was given that anyone demolished the building. In particular there was no evidence that it was done by the defendants. The workmen gave evidence that they never saw the first named defendant taking any steps to demolish the house. It is common case that some years later in 2001, Mr. Doohan had accidentally reversed his JCB into the plaintiff's then roofless house when he cleared the roadway of rubble between the hotel and the plaintiff's house on behalf of the local authority.

It was accepted that the first named defendant proceeded through the normal legal channels with Donegal County Council to clear the rocks, stones and debris from Presho's house to make the road passable.

Mr. Doohan wrote to Mr. Presho in reply to the latter's request to remove two white stones from his house site which were there without his permission as follows:

> "Dear Neville,
>
> Further to our conversation in the clubhouse last night I regret that I didn't come across the copy fax from Donegal County Council, but I can confirm that I cleared the road from rock, stones, and debris to make the road passable as instructed by Donegal County Council.
>
> Yours sincerely,
>
> Pat Doohan, 18/8/01."

3. The purported agreement of 4th October 2001

There was no evidence to support the allegation that Mr. Doohan drew up the purported agreement between Mr. Presho and himself on 4th October, 2001. The evidence points to the contrary in that Mr. Presho had asked Angela Duggan of Comharchuman Thorai, the island co-operative to prepare the document.

The agreement of 4th October, 2001, read as follows:

"We, the undersigned Neville Presho and P. Doohan do hereby this day 2001

enter into a binding agreement, where I P. Doohan will secure the land rights

to the area shown shaded, for Neville Presho and will assign to him the land, rights and ownership

of that area. In pursuance, I Neville Presho will simultaneously assign the land rights and ownership

of the land known as folio 13745F in O.S. 6 Donegal to Patrick Joseph Doohan of Óstán Thoraigh.

This is a straight swap transaction and does not involve any fanancial (*sic*) remuneration to either party.

Agreed at Tory on 4/10/2001. signed Neville Presho

signed P. Doohan.

witnessed Angela Duggan, runai, Comharchuman Thorai."

This was accompanied by a sketch signed by the three, the two parties and witnessed by Angela Duggan which showed a hatched round undetermined area beside the Community Centre.
Also included was a draft undated statement with the plaintiffs address in Hollywood, Co. Down and telephone numbers which stated as follows:

"It gives me great pleasure, as proprietor of Óstán Thoraigh to fully endorse Neville Presho's plans for a Tory visitor centre (illegible). His ideas and enthusiasm will ensure that Tory becomes a major tourist attraction in Ireland.

The ferry, the smooth operator TM will be 150 seat, state-of-the-art high speed wave (illegible) catamaran, designed to the specifications of skipper Jimmy Sweeney to suit the sea conditions around Tory. It will out trawl and reduce the time between Magherety to Tory from the current one hour to little under 20 minutes. In addition the ride in all sea conditions will be extremely stable.

I was involved in Mr. Presho's film 'Oilean' about life in Tory Island in 1976 and have enjoyed discussing ideas with him up to the present."

A further letter to the first name defendant from the plaintiff dated 20th June, 2003, from Hollywood, Co. Down read as follows:
"Dear Patrick Doohan,

This letter has been sent by registered mail.

When I met you on Tory Island in October, 2001, we both signed a legally binding document in which you were to acquire a site (marked) on the island, in exchange for you acquiring my house site.

As I had not heard from you since we signed that document on 4/10/01, I then wrote to you on 6/3/02 and again, received no response from you. You are hereby advised to expedite this matter within the next 21 days.

Failure to do so will result in this issue being taken out of my hands.

> Best wishes,
>
> Yours sincerely,
>
> Neville Presho."

A final letter dated 4th August, 2003, enclosed €100 which Mr. Doohan had lent Mr. Presho and referred to and enclosed a letter in relation to an unrelated matter.
Mr. Presho less than two weeks before the purported agreement gave notice of an application to the planning authority was published in the "Derry People" in "Donegal News" on Friday, September 21st, 2001. It read:

> "I, Neville Presho, am applying for planning permission for the erection of a two-storey replacement dwelling at Middletown, Tory Island."

No evidence was given in relation to any development of that application.
The agreement of 4th October, 2001 was signed by both Mr. Presho and Mr. Doohan. The evidence of the circumstances of its preparation and execution is bizarre and was referred to by two eminent psychiatrists as a manifestation of the plaintiff's mental impairment. The court, in its preliminary ruling of 3rd April, 2009, also referred to the agreement in relation to the plaintiff's inability to deal with his affairs. The evidence of Mr. Doohan was that while he signed it he did not think it would be binding. Neither party were legally represented.

The court accedes to the plaintiff's request and will declare the agreement of 4th October, 2001 to be null and void.

4. Circumstantial evidence

In assessing the evidence the Court has to identify the circumstantial evidence as well as the direct evidence given.

The circumstantial evidence of motive, capacity and opportunity depends on the reasonable inferences. The court is also entitled to consider the continuance of acts and the failure to give evidence or call witnesses (see Keane: *The Modern Law of Evidence*, 7th Ed. Oxford, 2008, 11-19).

Relevant facts are those which the existence or non-existence of a fact in issue may be inferred.

As already determined there is a lack of direct evidence in relation to critical facts alleged by the plaintiff. The absence of the plaintiff from Tory Island from 1988 to 1994, the delay in the Garda investigation of the initial complaint by Mr. McGinty, absence of a visit by the local authority until October 1994 and the delay in ascertaining and notifying Mr. Presho, then in New Zealand, on 29th April 1994, all contributed to the absence of direct and forensic evidence.

More telling was the lack of cooperation with the Garda investigation and the absence of corroborative evidence from neighbours.

The defendants benefited to some extent from the demolition of Mr. Presho's house. There was no evidence of lack of motive on their part to show the relative unlikelihood of their interest.

While the court accepts the removal by Mr. Doohan's JCB of debris from the road between the house and the hotel was authorised by the local authority, the removal of the remainder of the house required mechanical means. Mr. Doohan, as the owner of the only JCB on the island had the capacity and opportunity to remove the stones identified by Mr. Presho on the foreshore.

The court accepts that the demolition and removal of the house was gradual. The house did not disappear in an instant. The continuance of the process to a gravelled site infers planning and motivation. The court attaches particular importance to the photographic evidence of the uninterrupted view by the hotel of the harbour. Mr. Presho then put in evidence the superimposed outline of his house on that photograph which observed the direct view from the hotel. This was not objected to nor was he cross examined.

The court accepts the plaintiff's difficulties in getting evidence. The defendants' evidence denying the allegations was not corroborated other than in the use of the car park.

It is clear that in criminal law a combination of circumstances, no one of which could raise a reasonable conviction or more than a mere suspicion may, when taken together create a conclusion of guilt.

In *People (DPP) v. Nevin*, CCA, 14th March, 2003, the Court of Criminal Appeal approved Carroll J.'s direction to the jury as follows:

> "... to consider individually whether or not to accept each piece of circumstantial evidence, and to resolve any doubts arising therefrom in favour of the accused, given the presumption of innocence; thereafter, ... to consider the 'cumulative weight' of the circumstantial evidence, any inference it engendered in the case, (and) required to exclude the possibility of coincidence or fabrication before deciding to convict the accused."

Nevin involved a criminal protection requiring proof beyond reasonable doubt of circumstantial evidence.
The burden of proof in a civil case, such as this, is lower being the balance of probabilities.

5. The doctrine of *res ipsa loquitur*

The court further considers that the doctrine of *res ipsa locquitur* – the affair speaks for itself – while not entirely dispositive has some application to the case. Henchy J. in *Hanrahan v. Merck Sharp and Dohme* [1988] I.L.R.M 629 stated the following in relation to the doctrine of *res ipsa loquitur*: (emphasis added.)

> "The ordinary rule is that a person who alleges a particular tort must, in order to succeed, **prove** (save there are admissions) all the necessary ingredients of the tort and it is not for the defendant to disprove anything. Such exceptions as has been allowed to that general rule seem to be confined to cases where a particular element of the tort lies, or is deemed to lie, **pre-eminently within the defendant's knowledge, in which case the onus of proof as to that matter passes to the defendant.** Thus, in the tort of negligence, where damage has been caused to the plaintiff in circumstances in which such damage would not usually be caused without negligence on the part of the defendant, the rule of *res ipsa loquitur* will allow the act relied on to be evidence of negligence in the absence of proof by the defendant that it occurred without want of due care on his part. The rationale behind the shifting of the onus of proof to the defendant in such cases would appear to lie in the fact that it would be **palpably unfair to require a plaintiff to prove** something which is beyond his reach and which is peculiarly within the range of the defendant's capacity of proof." (emphasis added.)

While McMahon and Binchy in *Irish Law of Torts*, 2nd ed. (Dublin, Butterworths, 1989), are somewhat critical of this reasoning of Henchy J., the doctrine is applicable to the circumstances where motivation, capacity and opportunity of the defendants are considered. McMahon and Binchy point out:

"It is not the case that *res ipsa loquitur* may be invoked only where the evidence is more accessible to the defendant. Of course, proof of the elements of a case based on *res ipsa loquitur* frequently shows superior or exclusive knowledge on the part of the defendant as to how the accident occurred: of the nature of things, those in control of the instrumentality causing the injury are generally more likely to have such knowledge than their victims. But the *res ipsa loquitur* doctrine is neither reducible to, nor dependent on, this element ... **The whole point of the doctrine is to permit the making of an inferential conclusion that the defendant's negligent conduct caused the plaintiff's injury from the fact that (a) the thing causing the injury was under the defendant's control and (b) accidents such as the one befalling the plaintiff do not ordinarily happen if those in control exercise due care.**" (2nd ed. 1989 at 143) (emphasis added.)

The court is entitled to infer and is satisfied that it is probable that the first named defendants JCB, whether driven by that defendant or not, was the only "thing causing the injury".

6. Unjust enrichment

While not pleaded, the court considered, in addition to the circumstantial evidence, whether and if so, to what extent it was proper to consider restitution either as a *quasi* contractual or equitable remedy. The court allowed an opportunity to the plaintiff to consider an amendment. No such amendment was made, though the defendants made written submissions.

The court does not propose to address the matter.

6. Damages

The court is satisfied on the basis of the above analysis of the circumstantial evidence and the doctrine of *res ipsa loquitur* that the plaintiff is entitled to the damages for trespass and interference.

The final short hearing in relation to trespass and damages in relation to the path of the second defendant's septic tank and car parking on the plaintiff's site was heard on 13th July, 2009. The court considered the plaintiff's architect and valuer's affidavit together with the affidavits of Mr. Doohan of his valuer, Manus O'Ceallaigh, the affidavit's of his solicitor, Sean O'Canainn together with seven affidavits of inhabitants of Tory Island. The latter all said in like terms that they had not seen any cars parking where the plaintiff's house was nor where the hotel's septic tank was situate. Each said that they remembered well where the plaintiff's house was and where the septic tank for the hotel is. None of these deponents gave evidence in court as to what occurred to the plaintiff's house.

The affidavit of the first named defendant denied any involvement in the matters alleged in the plaintiff's statement of claim and referred to two questions which remained to be resolved.

The first was that of the septic tank. The first named defendant said that the hotel bought the land through Sean O'Canainn, their solicitor. Mr. O'Canainn in his affidavit referred to the pleadings and opposed any amendment thereto. He referred to the purchase of the land and easement in relation to the hotel's septic tank, the evidence of which had been given in the hearing in Letterkenny. He also referred to the planning permission obtained in relation to the septic tank.

In submissions made by Seamus O'Thuthail A.S., it was urged that Mr. Presho, the plaintiff, did not have prescriptive rights to the land which was not included in his folio. He had purchased the land in 1986 and the house had been unoccupied and had been destroyed in 1993 or 1994. Accordingly, the plaintiff had no prescriptive rights to the garden area or the septic tank due to the non-user of same.

It was further submitted that if there were damages, which was denied, then it was *damnum sine iniuria*.

Manus O'Ceallaigh, a valuer, referred to the affidavits already filed by Kevin V. Hyde, architect and Dermot J. Rainey, valuer. He said that the hotel did not use Mr. Presho's site for parking; there was ample parking around the hotel and only fifteen cars altogether on the island.

In submissions counsel referred to his valuation as being zero or insignificant insofar as the supply of parking is greater than the need.

Mr. O'Dualachain S.C. on behalf of Mr. Presho stressed the occurrence of trespass over a period of sixteen years. No licence to trespass could operate in favour of the second named defendant. The interests of the plaintiff in the land had to be upheld by the court which could draw inferences from common sense.

The Court is not satisfied that the property rights of the plaintiff in relation to the septic tank used by the plaintiff can be extinguished by non-user. While there was no argument in relation to the issue of the nature of easement acquired it would appear to have been an easement of necessity even though it was not covered by the folio. While no causation has been proved in relation to the destruction and demolition of the plaintiff's house it does not seem to be equitable that the second named defendant can enjoy its advantage and rely on the non-user of easement attaching to Mr. Presho's site. Whatever the cause of the destruction and demolition of the house it would seem to the Court that the legal entitlement of the plaintiff to rebuild the house, subject to planning permission, would include the use of the septic tank even if this is on land now transferred to the second named defendant.

Damages for trespass to the plaintiff's property in relation to access to the septic tank, as shown by Mr. Hyde, the architect on behalf of the plaintiff, can result in no significant damage, once the plaintiff is in the position to use the septic tank which benefited the site on which his house once stood.

The Court is not satisfied that the plaintiff has proven that there was trespass by way of parking of cars on the site.

The court in allowing the plaintiff claim at (a) and (d) of the Statement of Claim now considers the relief claimed at (b) (the restoration and rebuilding) and (c) (the removal of the septic tank, etc.).

The court is conscious of the delays in proceeding from the date of notification of the cause of action from 1994 to 2006, the absence of evidence of the state of the house prior to the fire and to the ambivalence of the plaintiff. The equitable remedy lies not in reinstatement but in the provision of a comparable dwelling on Tory Island or the open market value of a comparable dwelling on the island.

Section Three

9th November 2009

THE HIGH COURT

2006/4P

Monday the 9th day of November 2009

BEFORE MR JUSTICE MURPHY

BETWEEN

NEVILLE PRESHO

PLAINTIFF

AND

PATRICK DOOHAN AND OSTAN THORAIGH COMHLACHT TEORANTA

DEFENDANTS

This action being at hearing on the 2nd day of February 2009 the 3rd day of February 2009 the 4th day of February 2009 and the 5th day of February 2009 in the presence of Counsel for the Plaintiff and Counsel for the Defendants

Whereupon and on reading the Plenary Summons and Pleadings herein and the documents adduced in evidence and upon hearing the oral evidence of the witnesses whose names are set forth in the Schedule hereto and on hearing said Counsel respectively

The Court doth Reserve judgment herein and the matter coming before the Court again on the 3rd day of April 2009 the 8th day of May 2009 the 22nd day of May 2009 the 22nd day of June 2009 the 13th day of July 2009 the 17th day of July 2009 the 5th day of October 2009 the 2nd day of November 2009 and on this day

IT IS ORDERED AND ADJUDGED that the Plaintiff do recover against the Defendants the sum of €46,000 and costs of action when taxed and ascertained

THE HIGH COURT

And Counsel for the Defendants applying for a stay herein and on hearing said Counsel and Counsel for the Plaintiff IT IS ORDERED that this application do stand refused

DAVID NEENAN
REGISTRAR
9th April 2010

Michael Gillespie
Solicitors for the Plaintiff

Sean O Canainn
Solicitors for the Defendants

A COPY WHICH I ATTEST

Bridget Grehan

FOR REGISTRAR

Schedule hereinbefore referred to

For the Plaintiff	For the Defendants
Neville Presho	Supt. Eugene McGovern
Clifford Hailey	Eamonn O Neachtain
John McGinty	Brian McCaffrey
Sean Friel	Pat Doohan
Brian Rodden	Frankie MacGhionghaile
Charlie Cannon	Sean O Canainn
Kevin Hyde	Dermot Rainey
	Brian McLoughlin

Section Four

22nd October 2010

SUPREME COURT

Friday the 22nd day of October 2010   No. 139/10

BEFORE

MR JUSTICE FINNEGAN
MR JUSTICE O'DONNELL
MR JUSTICE MC KECHNIE
2006 No 4 P
BETWEEN

NEVILLE PRESHO
PLAINTIFF

AND

PATRICK DOOHAN AND
ÓSTAN THORAIGH COMHLACHT TEORANTA
DEFENDANTS

The Motion on the part of the Defendants pursuant to Notice of Motion herein dated the 17th day of September 2010 for a stay of execution on the judgment granted by Order of the High Court (Mr Justice Murphy) dated the 9th day of November 2009 pending the determination of the Defendants' appeal from the said Order coming on for hearing this day and upon reading the said Motion the Affidavit of Padraig Ó Dubhcháin herein filed on the 17th day of September 2010 and the Affidavit of Michael Gillespie filed on the 18th day of October 2010 and upon hearing Counsel for the Parties

IT IS ORDERED that execution of the said judgment be stayed for a period of six weeks conditional on the Defendant placing the sum of €46,000.00 on joint deposit Account in the name of both Solicitors within that time

And IT IS ORDERED that the costs be costs in the cause

Liberty to apply

MARY O'DONOGHUE
ASSISTANT REGISTRAR
Perfected 18th April 2011